The Sto_ ͜ __
Camberwell

by

Mary Boast

London Borough of Southwark

Neighbourhood History No.1

Southwark
Council

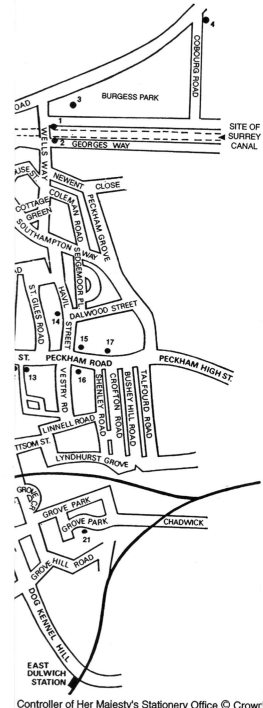

The Story of Camberwell

by

Mary Boast

London Borough of Southwark

Neighbourhood History No.1

isbn 0 905849 18 3

British Library Cataloguing in Publication data
A catalogue record for this book is available from the British Library

London Borough of Southwark
Local Studies Library
1996

1st edition 1972
Revised 1975 and 1980
Enlarged and rewritten 1996
Copyright London Borough of Southwark

Front cover: *Trams at Camberwell Green.*
From a painting by L.G.Davie at the South London Gallery.

Inside front cover: *View from Camberwell Grove.*
From William Thornton *History of London* 1784.

Inside back cover: Former baths and library, Wells Way, with the
Camberwell Beauty butterfly mural.

CONTENTS

Introduction

Index

INTRODUCTION AND ACKNOWLEDGEMENTS

This book is intended as an introduction to the history of the Camberwell area, now part of the London Borough of Southwark. It covers the area which has Camberwell Green at its centre and stretches roughly from Albany Road to Champion Hill, and from Flodden Road, Camberwell New Road, to Southampton Way. This area, the central part of the SE5 postcode defines today's Camberwell to most people. The book overlaps with other areas and other *Neighbourhood Histories*, those for Dulwich, Peckham and Walworth. In fact at one time Camberwell's parish boundaries extended to include Peckham and Dulwich. Part of the old parish of Camberwell is now in Lambeth and the book consequently occasionally strays over the present Borough boundary.

Camberwell's history is traced from its modest beginnings as a small farming village to its position today as a vibrant multi-cultural community central to Southwark and south London. In the intervening years it was a popular place of residence for the social elite of the early-modern period, and it underwent many stages of development; the grand Georgian, the less ostentatious Victorian and the very necessary post-war.

This book would not have been written without the hard work of many people. The staff of Southwark Local Studies Library, Stephen Humphrey, Margaret de Bristowe and Stephen Potter all provided the author with much assistance during the period of research and Stephen Humphrey again provided valuable suggestions during the later stages. Thanks are due to the staff at Lambeth Archives Department, and to the South London Gallery for permission to use paintings in their collection for the cover and two illustrations. Special thanks are due to the Camberwell Society and their present editor Tony Wilson, for use of much material from their newsletter, the *Camberwell Quarterly,* and for permission to reproduce the watercolour of Camberwell Grove. The text was typed by Jocelyn Heyford, the photographs prepared by Godfrey New and the book designed by Saundra O'Shea and Mic Clarke from Media & Design at Southwark Education & Leisure. Principally it would not have been possible without the dedication and meticulous work by Mary Boast who, during her period as Southwark's Local Studies Librarian and later in her work for the library on the *Neighbourhood Histories* has contributed as incomparable amount to our knowledge of the London Borough of Southwark area.

Len Reilly
Local Studies Librarian, Southwark
March 1996

1. EARLY DAYS

A country village

Camberwell Green is a pretty name, which sounds like the title of a song, but to most people today means just a bus stop, a busy traffic junction. It needs imagination to picture this small open space as it once was, the village green of Camberwell, one of London's very old villages, a place with a history and pattern of its own, a place where people have lived since long before William the Conqueror came to England in 1066.

It is not known for certain when people first made their homes here or how the village got its name. Obviously it was noted for its well. There were many wells in old Camberwell. One on the site of 56 Grove Park, was believed by some to have been the special "Camber Well". It was in use until about 150 years ago with a donkey going round drawing up the water. Several ideas have been put forward about the first part of the name Camberwell. Some old books say that "camber" meant crooked and that the water from Camberwell's well could cure crippled or crooked people. The *Oxford Dictionary of English Place Names*, however, says the name comes from an old English word meaning either cranes or jackdaws. Another suggestion has been made by the historian John Morris. In his book *The Age of Arthur*, he says Camberwell was a village of the ancient Britons, or "Welsh", who continued to live here after the Anglo-Saxon invasions. Camber would then come from the same word as "Cymru", the Welsh name for Wales. Walworth, the next village to Camberwell, means a farm of the Britons, or "Welsh". Wal comes from the Anglo-Saxon word for the same people.

The first known mention of Camberwell is in *Domesday Book*, the great survey of England made in 1086. It is written in Latin, with many abbreviations, but this is roughly what it says

> In Brixton Hundred Haimo holds Camberwell ... There is land for 5 ploughs, 2 in the lord's demesne. There are 22 villagers and 7 small-holders with land for 6 ploughs. There is a church, 63 acres of meadow, and woodland providing 60 pigs. In the time of King Edward [the Confessor] it was valued at £12, afterwards at £6, and now at £14.

1

Camberwell, then, 900 years ago, was just a village, or manor, with land for ploughing and growing corn, meadowland for cows, and woods where pigs could feed on acorns or beechnuts. It was a large enough village to have its own church, unlike Peckham, which is described separately in *Domesday Book.*

A few street or place names are reminders of Camberwell's early history. In 1086 the Lord of the Manor was Haimo, Sheriff of Surrey. His granddaughter, Mabel, married Robert, Earl of Gloucester, a son of King Henry I, and both Camberwell and Peckham became part of Robert's large estates, known as the Honour of Gloucester. Honor Oak was the southern boundary of his Camberwell lands and is still the boundary of the London Borough of Southwark. Much later the Duke of Buckingham inherited the Manor of Camberwell. He was executed in 1521, accused of treason against King Henry VIII, but for the next 300 years a large part of Camberwell was known as "Camberwell Buckingham". A map of 1739, in the British Museum, shows Buckingham Manor stretching north and south of the "Road from Camberwell to Peckham and Deptford." Dog Kennel Lane, now Grove Lane and Dog Kennel Hill, was its boundary with the Manor of Frerne, or Friern. Friern was a part of the large old Manor of Camberwell which had not belonged to the Duke of Buckingham. It had been given, in the Middle Ages, to Halliwell Priory, a convent of nuns in Shoreditch. In 1739, Friern Manor stretched west as far as what is now Denmark Hill and north to Camberwell Green. An old stone, inscribed "Friern Manor, 1791" is set in the brick gate-post of 30-32 Peckham Road, opposite the Town Hall. The name, Buckingham Manor, has been lost but Friern Road, East Dulwich, recalls the site of Friern Manor House. Dowlas Street, off Wells Way, North Camberwell, is a reminder of Dowlas (or D'Overdale) Manor, named after the family who held this part of Camberwell in the 14th century. What is now Cottage Green is marked on a map, made by John Rocque in 1745, as Dolles (Dowlas) Common. Milkwell Yard, off Denmark Hill, near Coldharbour Lane, was once part of the Manor of Milkwell, on the borders of Camberwell and Lambeth, described in 1609 as having "6 messuages (houses), 8 cottages, 5 barns, 5 gardens, 150 acres of land, 20 acres of pasture, and 30 acres of woodland".

For hundreds of years Camberwell remained a country village. Its few houses were clustered around the Green, the "High Street", now part of Camberwell Road and Denmark Hill, and Church Street, leading to St Giles, the parish church. There were not many other roads. Church Street

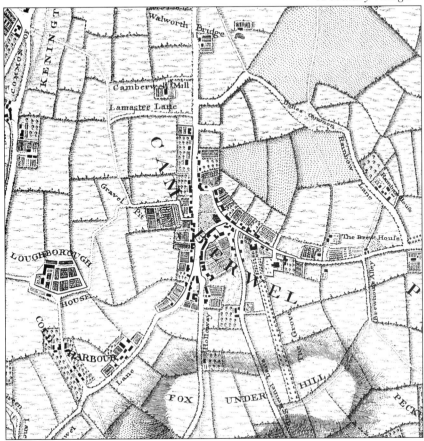

Camberwell, c. 1745
From John Rocque - A map of London and 10 miles round 1741-45.

continued as a lane, past fields to the village of Peckham, and so on to the main road to Kent, the Old Kent Road. In the other direction, Camberwell Lane, now Coldharbour Lane, led past the Manor of Coldharbour, to Brixton Hill, a route to the south. Cold Harbour, a name found in various parts of the country, suggests there was a cold shelter from the weather, for travellers and their animals, near the road, but away from the warmth of village inns. Dog Kennel Lane was another very old trackway. With its continuation, Lordship Lane, it was part of a route leading from London to the south of England. Camberwell Grove, known at one time as Walnut Tree Grove, was not originally a through road, but just an avenue of trees, leading to the top of the hill, from an old manor house which, until its demolition in 1776, blocked the Church Street end. Between Camberwell and Peckham,

Rainbow Lane, now Southampton Way, led to Walworth. It took its name from Rainbow House, a mansion remembered now only by Rainbow Street. Apart from these, there were only foot and field paths. It is interesting to follow one of these which is still a right-of-way, a short cut from St Giles's Church to the "High Street" via Churchyard Passage, and footpaths linking Camberwell Grove, Grove Lane, and Love Walk, perhaps a lovers' lane, for a pleasant stroll after the evening service. The route continues, across Denmark Hill and via Coldharbour Passage, to Coldharbour Lane. Camberwell Passage, between Camberwell Road and Camberwell New Road, near Camberwell Green, is all that remains of another old footpath which continued to the west. It was replaced in 1818 by Camberwell New Road. A painting of about 1815 shows a lady sitting on a stile at the entrance to the path.

> Camberwell lies in the Hundred of Brixton - about three miles from Blackfriars Bridge. The land is divided between arable, pasture and gardens; in the latter I include about 300 acres occupied by farmers and cowkeepers, cultivated to supply provision for their cattle. The soil is generally fertile and is much improved with manure which is easily procured from London.
>
> Daniel Lysons - *The Environs of London,* 1792.

The village of Camberwell supported itself from the surrounding fields. There were at least two windmills to grind corn into flour. Camberwell Mill, a boundary mark between Camberwell and Walworth, stood in Windmill Lane, now Bethwin Road. The Windmill pub nearby in Wyndham Road is a reminder of it. Wyndham Road itself was once Lamastee Lane, named probably from Lammas Day or Loaf Mass Day, 1st August, a very old harvest festival, when wheat and hay had been harvested and fences were taken down to allow animals to graze in the fields for the rest of the year. The other windmill was also in north Camberwell. Early pictures of St George's Church, Wells Way, show it in the background, south east of the church. Grapes may have grown on the slopes of what is now Camberwell Grove. In 1717 a piece of land called the Vineyard was given to enlarge St Giles churchyard. Much land was probably just rough pasture, for example, the Bushey Hyll mentioned in deeds of the 16th century, which has given its name to Bushey Hill Road. Barley, used in making beer, was also grown in Camberwell. Two women brewsters are recorded as early as 1275. There was a brewhouse at what is now 37 Peckham Road by 1745, which remained the site of a brewery until the 1920s.

Before modern transport London obtained its fresh food from nearby villages, such as Camberwell. This trade grew as London expanded and its population increased. Manning and Bray's *History of Surrey*, published in 1809, says of Camberwell "In the pasture a great number of cows are kept which not only supply the inhabitants of this place with milk but furnish a good deal for London." At that time much of the land between Camberwell Green and Kennington was orchards belonging to the Camberwell Green Farm, owned then by the Minet family who had a large estate, mainly in Lambeth. A plan of 1789 shows the farmhouse facing the Green, with farmyards, carthouse, barns and stables. Myatt's Fields, Lambeth, now a park, took their name from a market gardener famous for his strawberries. Land north of Camberwell Green was acquired about 1800 by Robert Edmonds, another prosperous market gardener.

Tenpenny's Great Osier Farm, in Coldharbour Lane, produced osiers, a type of willow. Its shoots were used for making baskets to take the fruit to market. The Camberwell Beauty butterfly, which feeds on willows, got its name from being seen, in 1748, for the first time in England, near this farm. Needless to say it has long since vanished from Camberwell, though attempts have been made to reintroduce it. With its three-inch wide claret red wings, bordered with blue spots and white edging, it would be a welcome summer sight. Failing the real thing, at least there is its picture, in ceramic tiles over the Butterfly Walk Shopping Centre, Denmark Hill, and also on the outside of the former Camberwell Baths, Wells Way.

Old St Giles, church and parish

The present St Giles's Church, Peckham Road, was erected in 1844. Its tall spire can be seen almost anywhere in Camberwell. It replaces a much older church, destroyed by fire, which would have been even more the most noticeable building in the village of Camberwell. For local people it was all important, being their parish church, their only place, then, for the worship of God, and also the centre of their village life.

There has been a Christian church on this site for at least a thousand years. The Saxon church which William the Conqueror's men saw when they came to make Domesday Book was probably built of wood. In 1152 the Lord of the Manor, William, Earl of Gloucester, had it rebuilt in stone and gave it to "God and the monks of St Saviour, Bermondsey". Bermondsey Abbey, on the site of Abbey Street, off Tower Bridge Road, had the right of appointing the vicars of St Giles until the time of King Henry VIII.

St Giles, to whom the church is dedicated, is said to have been a hermit who lived in a cave in the south of France about 700 AD. He had a pet deer. Stories say he was accidentally wounded by an arrow when he had the deer in his arms to protect her from the huntsmen. A small figure of St Giles, with the deer, watches over the entrance to the present church. Prosser's history of the church, published in 1827, suggested that it was dedicated to him because of the Camber Well which, the author believed, meant well of the crooked or disabled. St Giles was the patron saint of crippled and sick people.

The fire which destroyed the old church on 7th February, 1841 was so fierce that stained glass melted and stone crumbled to powder; despite this, there are still some links with it in the present church. Near the entrance is a list of vicars going back to 1290. At the east end there are 600-year old carved stone sedilia, or priests' seats, and a stone piscina, a bowl for washing the Communion cups, saved from the ruins of the old church. Outside the Youth Centre in Benhill Road are other relics of the stonework, made into a summer-house in what used to be the vicarage garden. The walls of the old church were lined with memorials in stone or brass. Some of the brasses were saved from the fire and are on display in the south transept of the present church. The earliest is that of Richard Skinner, who is reckoned to have died in 1493. There are also fine memorials, dating from the Tudor

John Bowyer and family, 1570
Brass memorial at St Giles's church

period, to John Scott and John Bowyer. Both families played an important part in Camberwell's history.

The memorials and tombstones in St Giles's churchyard were cleared in 1939 to make a garden. Among those buried here were James Blake who sailed with Captain Cook, and Mary Wesley, wife of John Wesley, founder of Methodism.

The registers of baptisms, marriages and burials in St Giles, which date from 1558, the year Elizabeth I became queen, are now in the Greater London Record Office. From them much can be learnt about Camberwell and its people. For example, the burial register shows that, sadly, over a hundred people in this village died of the Great Plague of London in 1665, and many also in earlier outbreaks in 1603 and 1625.

St Giles was a very large parish. Parishioners came to church, mostly on foot, from the whole of Dulwich and Peckham, as well as Camberwell, for, in the early days, neither of these hamlets had churches of their own. The boundaries of the old parish stretched from a stream on the line of Boundary Lane, Walworth Road, in the north, to Sydenham Hill in the south and from Denmark Hill in the west to beyond Old Kent Road in the east. Some old boundary posts can still be found, for example, outside 36 Champion Hill, 169 Denmark Hill, and on One Tree Hill, where an oak tree, replacing the earlier "Honor Oak" also marks the ancient boundary. In the past it was the custom, once a year, to perambulate, or walk round, the boundaries of the parish. According to Blanch, the Camberwell historian, "no perambulation was complete without the singing of the 104th psalm under the shadow of the Oak of Honour Hill". With only some minor changes the old parish boundaries became the boundaries of the new Borough of Camberwell in 1900.

It was at the old St Giles's Church that organised local government for Camberwell began. On 2nd June, 1674, a general meeting of parishioners was held in the church, where, according to the minutes, "it was voted that a certain number of the constant inhabitants should be nominated - - to meet once a month in the parish church to consult with the minister and parish officers about the affairs of the parish - - and to communicate from time to time what they have debated of to a general meeting of parishioners" The committee nominated, like those in other parishes, was known as the Vestry, because it met, originally, in the vestry of the church. St Giles's

Vestry was the local government for Camberwell until 1900, when it was replaced by a Borough Council.

One of the Vestry's duties was to look after its own poor people, the old, the sick and those who had no work. For this a poor rate was collected from property owners and then distributed to the poor. Records of payments date from the 1670s, for example

1679 - To a poor woman who was burnt out - 6 pence
1694 - For nursing the child that was found under the
     haystack at Walworth Bridge - 5 shillings
1700 - Gave to Hugh Moulsey that was out of work and like to fall
     into despair - 3 shillings and 6 pence

Not all these expenses came out of the rates as other receipts show other sources of income such as

1695 - From men sitting in ye ale houses drinking in sermon time -
     3 shillings and 6 pence

Some people also left lands or money to help the poor. Thanks to them, loaves of bread were given out to very poor people in church on Sundays and winter coats at Christmas.

In 1727, the Camberwell Vestry, "finding the number of their poor daily increasing", decided on another way of dealing with some of them. Like other parishes at the time, they erected a workhouse, a small building at the corner of Workhouse Lane, now Havil Street (on the opposite corner from the present Town Hall). Here the poor and unemployed had to live under the charge of a workhouse master who set to work, any capable of working, winding silk, and making purses, gloves and other small items.

The Vestry also dealt with other village matters, for example, law and order, public safety, upkeep of the highways and the control of nuisances. Wrongdoers in the village were condemned to sit in the stocks. These were in Peckham Road, outside the workhouse, where they could be seen by every passer-by. Those awaiting trial or imprisonment were held in the cage, a small building with barred windows, on the site of 33 Denmark Hill, in what was the yard of the Joiners' Arms. Next door to it was a watchhouse for the watchmen who went about the village streets at night, before there was any Metropolitan Police service, seeing that all was well. If a fire broke out, Camberwell had its own fire engine, or parish squirt, a hosepipe on a barrow, which was kept in the engine house, a small building next door to the workhouse, replaced about 1809 by a new engine house facing the north side of Camberwell Green. There were also traffic problems. In 1797 residents were much troubled by pigs being allowed to "range at large in the roads". Five shillings' reward was paid for information as to their owners. Payments were also made for the eradication of agricultural pests such as caterpillars, hedghogs, polecats and sparrows. Three pence a dozen was paid for sparrow heads and the now nearly extinct polecat commanded a shilling for each one destroyed.

The first known school in Camberwell was founded in 1615 by Edward Wilson, Vicar of St Giles. Wilson's Grammar School stood just to the east of the old church. According to the founder's rules, the scholars were to be Camberwell boys, including twelve children of poor parents, who were taught free. School hours were long, ten hours a day in summer, including Saturdays, and eight in winter when the boys had to take candles to do their lessons. On Thursdays they had a half day's holiday. On Sundays they went to church where the north gallery was reserved for them. The school finally left Camberwell in 1975. The Greencoat School, facing the north side of Camberwell Green, was a Charity School for poor boys and girls. The inscription on the outside of the building read "Erected to the Glory of God and the honour of the Church of England by Henry Cornelisen, Esquire, in 1721". On either side of this inscription were two little stone figures of a boy and girl in the Greencoat uniform. Here, at first, just 15 boys and 15 girls aged 7-12 had the chance of learning to read and write. They were given their green uniform and when they left school it was dyed black and they were allowed to keep it. They were also given Bibles and prizes for good behaviour. It seems to have been a kindly school. There are even records of an early school outing. In 1714, when George I arrived to be crowned king, stands and refreshments in the streets of London were provided for the children to see the procession. Wealthy local people supported the school with their subscriptions and every year there was a special sermon at St Giles when a collection for it was taken. Rebuilt in 1872, the school survived until World War II.

Great houses and great families

Castlemead, an eighteen storey block of flats, now dominates the skyline on the west side of Camberwell Road. Two hundred years ago this was approximately the site of another impressive building, though only three storeys high, the mansion of the Lords of the Manor, the Bowyer family. In those days the village of Camberwell had a number of grand houses with large landed estates. Bowyer House was one of the oldest of these. The family had been in Camberwell since 1550 when John Bowyer of Somerset, a London lawyer, married the wealthy Elizabeth Draper. Her father had acquired the Manor of Camberwell Friern after the dissolution of the monasteries. John Bowyer bought beautiful materials to make wedding clothes for his bride "4 ells of tawney taffeta for a Venyce gowne, one yard and a half quarter of scarlett for a pety cote with plites". They had a house by Camberwell Green with fine silver on their dinner table. On their brass memorial in St Giles's Church they are pictured together with their eleven children, all wearing ruffs, in fashion at the time. The eldest son inherited Friern Manor and was made Sir Edmond Bowyer. On September 1st, 1657 John Evelyn visited Bowyer House, Camberwell Road, where the Lord of the Manor was by now living. In his famous diary he wrote, "visited Sir Edmond Bowyer (nephew of the first Sir Edmond) at his melancholie seat at Camberwell. He has a very pretty grove of oaks and hedges of yew in his garden, and a handsome row of tall elms before his court" In time the Bowyer family came to own a great deal of Camberwell and also Peckham and East Dulwich, not only Friern Manor, but also parts of Camberwell Buckingham and Milkwell Manor. Their fields stretched from Kennington Common (now Kennington Park) to Old Kent Road. On the map dated 1739 the owner of the estate is entitled Joseph Windham (Wyndham) Ash Esq., and on another of 1830 the owner is Sir Thomas Smyth, but it was the same family. The Bowyers often had no sons, and the estate was inherited through women. Bowyer House was finally demolished in 1861 to make way for the railway. By then the Bowyer lands had mostly been sold for building. Only the street names, Wyndham Road and Bowyer Place, are reminders of this great estate.

At the foot of Camberwell Grove and Grove Lane was another old Manor House, home of the Lords of the Manor of Camberwell Buckingham, the Scotts. John Scott was "one of the Barons of the King's Exchequer", in the time of King Henry VIII and was granted the manor after the execution of the Duke of Buckingham. The brass in St Giles's Church shows him and his wife, Elizabeth, kneeling at prayer and there is also a brass of their son, Edward. Later owners of the manor were the Cock family. The estate was eventually sold up in 1776 and the Manor House, already partly in ruins, was demolished.

The Old House on the Green, as it was known, faced the south side of Camberwell Green. Built in 1709, on the site of an even earlier house, it had a large pond in front of it and gardens behind stretching as far as what is now Daneville Road. It was said to have had a magnificent hall decorated by Sir James Thornhill, the artist responsible for the interior of the dome of St Paul's. The Old House was demolished in 1852 to build the Wren Road Church, itself now replaced by the new flats called The Colonades. Kwiksave, 30 Denmark Hill, is on the site of another old mansion, Northampton House, demolished in 1908, once a town residence of the Earl of Northampton.

Street names such as De Crespigny Park, Champion Park, Champion Hill and Champion Grove are all reminders of the beautiful country estate of the de Crespigny family which stretched right from Love Walk to the foot of Dog Kennel Hill. The old brick wall on the south side of Love Walk was once part of its boundary wall and other parts may be seen on the east side of Champion Hill. The family were Huguenots, French Protestants, who escaped to England in 1685, to avoid persecution for their religious beliefs. They went first to Marylebone and moved to the de Crespigny mansion, Champion Lodge, at the corner of Love Walk and Denmark Hill, Camberwell, in 1741. Here, William Claude Champion de Crespigny, who inherited the estate in 1765, and his talented wife, Mary, a writer and poet, entertained royalty and he was made a baronet. On a beautiful sunny day, 22nd June, 1804, they held a Fete Champetre, a grand garden party, for 500 guests, including the Prince of Wales, the future King George IV. The *Gentleman's Magazine* made it sound rather like the court of Queen Marie Antoinette at Versailles before the French Revolution, "groups of ladies, with rakes and light implements of rural employment danced round a garland of rich festoons of foliage and flowers, while music of different kinds in tune reverberated on the ear". In the house "the tables were loaded with the richest refreshments", including ices. As this was long before refrigeration, there must have been an icehouse somewhere in the grounds. The day ended with a "sportive dance" on the lawn by the light of a clear full moon. Five years later Sir Claude and Lady Mary moved away from

Camberwell. Stone memorials to them are set against the south wall of St Giles's Churchyard. Champion Lodge was demolished in 1841. Windsor Walk is named after Lady Sarah Windsor, wife of Sir Claude's son, William, and Maldon Close after a later family residence in Maldon, Essex. The title has been extinct since 1952 but members of the family still proudly carry on the name.

Two hundred years ago, Grove Hill, a mansion and estate at the top of Camberwell Grove, was widely famed. It was the home, from 1779-1810, of the great doctor, John Coakley Lettsom. Born in the West Indies, but educated in England, he had grown rich treating patients in the West Indies and London and had bought part of the Manor of Camberwell Buckingham when it was sold up. He was a well known character. People even recited a little verse about him,

> When any sick to me apply
> I physics, bleeds and sweats 'em
> If after that they choose to die
> Why verily - - -
> I Lettsom

But this verse does not give a fair idea of him. As a Quaker, a member of the Religious Society of Friends, Lettsom was noted for his generosity and kindness to poor people, and for many far-sighted charitable works. He was a founder of the Medical Society of London and the Royal Humane Society. He championed new methods of reviving people who had nearly drowned and vaccination against small-pox, a terrible scourge at that time. He founded the first General Dispensary in London for poor sick people and also a Sea Bathing Hospital at Margate.

He had chosen Grove Hill for his residence because it was near enough to town for his professional duties and yet, as he said, it caught the healthy breezes blowing from the south. His large Villa had one whole wing for a museum of coins, shells, and minerals, and a library of 6,000 volumes. The estate stretched from the top of the hill down to the present Lettsom Street. Near the house a kitchen garden, an orchard and hothouses provided vegetables and fruit, including apricots, peaches, grapes, figs and mulberries. Dr Lettsom was a keen naturalist and his estate had many interesting plants from other lands, all labelled with their Latin and English names. It also had other attractions, statues like those of ancient Greece and Rome, and a Temple of the Sybils, with a turret which gave wonderful views of the Thames from Lambeth to Limehouse. Clever use was made of a natural spring which was said to have been the one which fed the original Camber Well. It supplied a large brick reservoir which provided piped water for the estate and for a boating lake with a fountain in the middle. Overlooking this was the picturesque Fountain Cottage and weeping willow trees. Many distinguished visitors came to Grove Hill and wrote in praise of it. Thomas Maurice ended his long descriptive poem with these lines,

> Such are the soft enchanting scenes displayed
> In all the blended charms of light and shade
> At Camberwell's fair grove and verdant brow,
> The loveliest Surrey's lofty hills can show.

Most of the statues, plaques, and other artistic features of Grove Hill were made of Coade stone. This fashionable artificial stone was produced at Mrs Elizabeth Coade's factory, near the present site of the Festival Hall. Its best known piece, for Londoners, is the lion at the south end of Westminster Bridge. Mrs Coade died in Camberwell in 1821, possibly at the home of a relative, in Camberwell Grove.

Dr Lettsom's villa; south view; c. 1800

Unfortunately, Lettsom's generosity meant that by 1810 he had to sell up and leave Grove Hill. The estate was soon built over. The lake and Fountain

Cottage disappeared when the railway came. The Villa itself was demolished in the 1890s. 9-12 Grove Park cover the site. Two houses that Dr Lettsom would have known are still lived in today. 8 Grove Park, built in the 1770s, was once the residence of his next door neighbour and friend, Colonel Henry Smith. The rear view of it from Lettsom Gardens is particularly fine, a real country mansion in the heart of Camberwell. The other house is The Hermitage, 220 Camberwell Grove, a pretty cottage, or cottage orné, a little like his Fountain Cottage. A thatched cottage at 94 Camberwell Grove survived until World War II. Lettsom is now the name of a council housing estate.

There is however a small part of Lettsom's land which has not been built on, Lettsom Gardens, between Grove Park and Grove Hill Road, preserved thanks to the efforts of local people, the Lettsom Gardens Association. It has grass and woodland with some trees such as mulberries, probably descended from those planted by Dr Lettsom's gardeners. It is a wildlife haven for flowers, butterflies, birds and small creatures such as the Camberwell hedgehogs. Next to it are allotments worked by the Camberwell Gardens Guild. The great doctor would surely have been pleased to see such use made of the last remnant of his beautiful estate.

Camberwell Fair and other attractions

This is an invitation song,
For the London lads and lasses,
Camberwell Fair, I now declare,
All others now surpasses;
Both young and old, the spruce and gay,
The clown and beau's invited,
With rural scenes upon the Green,
You are sure to be delighted.

From *Camberwell Fair New Revived, 1795.*

The event of the year was Camberwell Fair held annually on Camberwell Green at the end of August, finishing on 1st September, the feast day of St Giles. In the Middle Ages it lasted three weeks and, like other fairs, then, would have been a chance for merchants to trade and for local people to buy goods they could not produce on their own lands. In 1279 the Lord of the Manor, Gilbert de Clare, Earl of Gloucester, claimed the privilege of holding the assize of ale and bread, that is, setting their price, "in his vill of Camberwell", presumably at the time of the fair. Later the fair only lasted three days and became just a time for entertainment. Attractions included melodramas at Richardson's Theatre set up in the centre of the Green, and Wombwell's Menagerie where lions and other wild beasts were on show. In the evening hundreds of fairy lamps lit up the Green, bands played and people danced. There were stalls all along Camberwell Road as far as the toll-gate (about the present junction with Westmoreland Road), selling plenty to eat from gingerbread to oysters, and -

> Browsy Nan in her dripping pan,
> Has sausages to sell too,
> But as each link she knew must stink,
> She's garnished them with mustard,
> And some who eat thought them as sweet,
> As tho' they had eat a custard.

It was not just the village boys and girls who went to the Fair. It attracted the London lads and lasses. Before rail or motor transport they could only go as far as places like Camberwell for a day's outing from the crowded city. A handbill dated 1842 advertises a four in hand drag (a four horse coach) which ran "six times a day to convey the aristocracy from Covent Garden" and there were go-carts from the Elephant and Castle. Unfortunately, as London grew and Walworth and Camberwell became built up, the Fair attracted, as fairs often do, what Blanch called, "a horde of nomadic thieves, coarse men and lewd women". The Camberwell Vestry had to employ twelve Bow Street runners, officers from the Bow Street magistrates, to keep the peace during the Camberwell and Peckham fairs. Perhaps there was good reason for building the first Camberwell Police Station at the corner of Camberwell Road and Camberwell New Road, overlooking the Green! Peckham Fair was abolished in 1827. A committee of local residents finally secured the abolition of Camberwell Fair in 1855. The site was then handed over to the Vestry to ensure that Camberwell's ancient village green remained forever as an open space.

Old Camberwell had many attractions, not only at fair time, but throughout the year, for the citizens of London. Before there were any houses in Camberwell Grove, the Grove House was already a famous tavern with tea gardens and a bowling green. In 1801, it was described it as "a large genteel house, well adapted as a place of public entertainment, and much frequented by genteel companies". It was the meeting place in the 1750s of the exclusive Camberwell Club, which had members from such leading families as the de Crespignys and the Bowyers. Attached to the Grove House was Camberwell Hall, scene of fashionable balls. Charles Dickens, in his *Sketches by Boz*, pictured one of them, attended by the Maldertons, two sisters who lived at "Oak Lodge, Camberwell". The elder Miss Malderton, aged 28 and desperately hoping to find herself an aristocratic husband, was to be sadly disappointed in Horatio Sparkins, the charming young man she met there! The Grove House Tavern, rebuilt in 1927, is still very much in business. Camberwell Hall, dated 1748, has recently been well restored as a private residence and school.

At the top of Denmark Hill, where the Fox on the Hill now stands, there was, for a few years, one of Camberwell's grandest places of entertainment. This was Denmark Hall, from which Denmark Hill takes its name. It was erected by Luke Lightfoot and was so called in honour of the King of

Camberwell Fair, c. 1850
From an oil painting at the South London Gallery

Denmark who was on a visit to this country. (King Christian VII visited England in 1768.) When it was first opened, it was much frequented by large parties from London, and contained one of the largest rooms in England - over 100 feet long and 30 feet wide.

Lightfoot himself is remembered for quite another reason. He was especially skilled in the art of wood carving, for which he had workshops in Gravel Lane, now Great Suffolk Street, and Blackman Street, now part of Borough High Street, both in north Southwark. His finest work may still be seen at Claydon House, a National Trust mansion in Buckinghamshire, where it is described as "the most perfect expression of Rococo decoration in England". If Denmark Hall once had such carving, unfortunately it did not survive. The building did not pay as a place of entertainment. It was converted into private houses and later demolished.

Other one-time attractions have also disappeared without trace. In Wyndham Road, ladies and gentlemen could enjoy the delights of the Royal Flora Gardens, a place to rival London's more famous pleasure gardens, such as Vauxhall and Ranelagh, with its shady avenues, statuary, grottoes, fountains, waterfalls, a maze like Hampton Court, and a ballroom with a full orchestra. And all this for an admission fee of only sixpence! Sadly, the Flora Gardens were built over in 1863. The old Rosemary Branch Tavern in Southampton Way was also a place for a good day out. It had grounds for cricket, horse racing, and other sports, until these too gave way to streets and houses.

The pleasant country inns around the Green have proved the longest lasting attractions of Camberwell. Rebuilt, they have become the pubs of today. A Father Redcap and also a Mother Redcap, next door, are marked on the map of 1739. There was an inn called the Artichoke in Camberwell Church Street as early as 1744. The Joiners' Arms, Denmark Hill, goes back over 200 years and so did the Tiger, now renamed the Silver Buckle. Between them were the Golden Lion and the Cock, only demolished about ten years ago to build the Shopping Centre.

2. INTO THE MODERN ERA

Georgian and early Victorian Camberwell

> The village, (Camberwell), has been uniformly increasing and at no period so rapidly as within the last ten years. It has the reputation of being healthy and is a very commodious situation for those persons who, from inclination, or for the benefit of the air, - - prefer a country residence, though business calls them daily to the metropolis.

Daniel Lysons - *The environs of London,* 1792

Along each of the main roads that meet at Camberwell Green - Camberwell Road, Camberwell Church Street, and Camberwell New Road - are some houses that have been there for about two hundred years. They are part of Camberwell's Georgian heritage, built during the reigns of King George III and George IV. Once these roads were lined with similar houses. They date from a time when Camberwell first began to develop from a country village into a suburb of London. When new, these elegant houses were each occupied by just one family, with living-in servants, obviously fairly wealthy people. They had come to live here at that time because London was expanding and because new bridges over the Thames, Westminster, Blackfriars, Vauxhall and Southwark Bridge, and improved roads leading to them, had made it easier for prosperous business and professional gentlemen to live away from their work and travel daily into town. For early commuters who could afford the time, and expense, of horse-drawn coach or private carriage, Camberwell was now within easy reach of the City or Westminster.

In Camberwell Road, the best preserved Georgian houses, on the east side, are 117-155. Notice especially the doorways and the fanlights above them. Before streets were numbered, each terrace or individual house had a name. 131, now occupied by Cambridge House, was once part of the terrace called Addington Place. The old name may still be seen on the corner of the building. It was probably named after Henry Addington, Prime Minister, 1801-4. In Addington Square, leading off Addington Place, you escape the traffic noise and find something of the peace and quiet there must have been throughout Camberwell for the first occupants of these houses. They are built round three sides of a garden. Two fine individual houses, 8 and 48, date from about 1810. The square was complete before 1855. On the north side, now an entrance to Burgess Park, early residents had a swimming bath. It matched in height the smaller houses on the south side of the square. On the west side of Camberwell Road, opposite Addington Place, is another Georgian terrace. No. 86, now an electrical suppliers, was originally the premises of Garland and Fieldwick, who were builders and stonemasons, when Camberwell was first being developed. The fine plaques above the entrance are of Coade stone, said to have come from Dr Lettsom's house. Other old houses on Camberwell Road are not so well cared for. They are hidden behind shops which have been built in what were once their long front gardens. They are best seen from across the road, or from the top of a bus. One example is Bowyer Place behind 156-8 Camberwell Road. 14-15 Camberwell Green, now a doctors' surgery, and 323 Camberwell New Road nearby, are crowded in by later buildings.

The Crescent, Camberwell Grove.
From a sale catalogue, 1836

Many local people have been married at one of the Georgian houses in Peckham Road. No. 34, now the Registrar's Office, is part of a terrace of twelve houses built about 1790. It still has its cobbled courtyard with an old lampstandard. Lucas Gardens, the public park behind the terrace, was formed from the long back gardens of these houses. Other Georgian buildings across the road are now an extension to the Town Hall. Camberwell New Road was built a little later. It was a new road in 1818, built to link Camberwell with Vauxhall Bridge, opened in 1816. Many of the houses are now being restored, revealing again their light brickwork which had been hidden by 170 years of London's soot and grime. There has been a pub named the William IV ever since he was king, 1830-37.

In all the main roads, naturally, with time, much has changed, but tree-lined Camberwell Grove and Grove Lane are streets which retain a great deal of the glory of their Georgian architecture, some of the best in the London area. The building up of Camberwell Grove and Grove Lane began after 1776 when the Manor of Camberwell Buckingham was sold and the old manor house demolished, thus opening up the entrance to the Grove from Camberwell Church Street and making it a public road. Before there was piped water or proper sewage this was an especially healthy area, set on a hillside, so drainage was good, and with fresh water from the springs which had fed the original Camber Well. The Chamberlains were typical of those who came to live here. In 1834 they moved to 188 Camberwell Grove from their house in the City where their family had been in business for at least a hundred years. Their son, Joseph, the future statesman, was born there in 1836, the first of the family not to be "born over the shop". For a year, until the family moved away, he attended the small private school kept by Miss Charlotte and Miss Harriet Pace a few doors away.

The elegant and well proportioned Georgian houses in Camberwell Grove have the main rooms on the first floor, with long windows giving extra light and views over front and back gardens. There are often basements where the servants cooked the meals and attics where they slept, but the houses are not all exactly alike. There is an interesting variety. Some are two, others three, or four, storeys high. They were not all built at the same time or by the same builders. The earliest terraces, near the foot of Camberwell Grove on the east side, 33-45 and 79-85, date from the 1770s - 1780s when Dr Lettsom still owned the land at the top of the hill. William Whitten, a solicitor, who bought Lettsom's estate, built 169-183, "Grove Crescent", in 1819. The Grove Chapel was built the same year. Its classical style fits in well with neighbouring houses. Some of the oldest houses in Grove Lane are 18-62, on the west side, set back behind extra long front gardens, and known in 1790 as Queen's Row. On the other side of the road are some interesting individual houses, for example, 65a White Cottage, 83 Cliftonville, built about 1820 in the Gothic style with pointed windows, and 201 Spring Mount, dated 1824.

Some of Camberwell's grandest Georgian houses were built at the top of Champion Hill, on land that belonged to Sir Claude Champion de Crespigny. Their occupants would obviously have been fitting neighbours for him. The largest to survive is 23 Champion Hill, probably designed about 1790 by Michael Searles, well known architect of Surrey Square, off Old Kent Road, and of the Paragon, Blackheath. Champion Lodge, 29 Champion Hill, once the dower house of the de Crespignys, and Champion Cottage, 47, are also two very attractive houses. In the 1830s and 40s, the early years of Queen Victoria's reign, houses for prosperous people were still being built on the de Crespigny estate, for example, the west side of Champion Grove. 93-99 Denmark Hill, too large for modern families, have recently been restored by the Orbit Housing Association for King's College Hospital.

In 1848 the Lettsom estate was bought by William Chadwick, who had made his fortune mainly as a railway engineer, at a time when railways were first being constructed in the London area. Chadwick moved into 8, once the home of Colonel Henry Smith, and soon began the development of the rest of Grove Park, the earliest houses being 13, 14 and 129, all built before 1862. Until about 1906 the houses of Grove Park looked on to a central garden but this is now also covered by houses. It is easy to see that Grove Park was once an exclusive neighbourhood. At the entrance is the old lodge, 126, where in the 1880s the lodge-keeper, Old Scrivens, was still keeping an eye on visitors and charging them a penny to walk through to Peckham! Champion Hill, similarly, had its residents' association and gates to keep out unwanted strangers.

Nearly all the houses mentioned above are now listed buildings, on the Department of the Environment's *List of buildings of special architectural or historic interest.*

North Camberwell - the early years

East from Camberwell Road is a vast green open space, stretching all the way to Old Kent Road. As old maps show, this is how the area would have been two hundred years ago, before development began. Then it was used for food production, mainly as market gardens. Now it is Burgess Park. Strangers might think this land had never been built on. Local residents with long memories know better. In under two centuries a whole townscape has come and gone.

The Camberwell Road entrance to Burgess Park was once under water. It was the western end of the Grand Surrey Canal, constructed 1801-1811, closed and filled in 1970. In the days before rail or motor transport, the building materials needed for the development of Camberwell, especially timber, could be carried more easily and cheaply by boat than by horse and cart. The canal made it possible for barges with sails, or drawn by horses plodding along the towpath, to bring goods landed at the docks of Rotherhithe as far inland as Camberwell Road. Industries sprang up along the canal banks, notably lime kilns for heating the limestone, brought by barge, and converting it into the quick lime needed for cement. One kiln has actually been left standing in Burgess Park, but it is difficult to picture it as it once was, part of the busy lime works of E R Burtt & Sons, here from 1816 until the 1960s, a hive of industry, with several smoking kilns, other large buildings, and a landing place on the north bank of the canal.

For North Camberwell the canal was all important. Its development began as almost a separate village, mainly for those working on or around the canal. It was a place of small streets and mostly small, two storey houses, less grand than the Georgian terraces on the main roads. Albany New Road, linking Camberwell Road with Old Kent Road, Southampton Street (now Southampton Way), Edmund Street, Park Street (now Parkhouse Street) and Cottage Green are all shown on maps of the 1820s. By 1824 the neighbourhood had its own parish church, St George's, Wells Way, a fine building with room for 2,000 people. The way to the church was New Church Road. Its vicarage was the Gothic style house just north of the present vicarage. To the north of the church was the canal, crossed by a hump-backed bridge, with a brewery on the other side. To the east of the church were brick kilns.

The Grand Surrey Canal with St George's Church, 1934

Apart from the old church building, North Camberwell still has a few other charming survivals of its very early years, that make it well worth exploring. 97-111 Wells Way and 28-52 Havil Street are examples of the type of houses which would once have lined these streets. Collingwood House, 23 Cottage Green, a listed building, must once have housed one of the neighbourhood's more affluent residents, as also the four-storey, 71-77 Southampton Way. When North Camberwell first began to develop there was no piped water to individual houses. Some houses, such as 199 - 201 Southampton Way could have used the old pump still to be seen at the junction with Peckham Grove. Later the pump became a lamp-standard and beside of it was set a horse trough, with also a tap and cup for their drivers and a low trough for dogs. It has the inscription "Blessed are the pitiful - the work of St Luke's Band of Mercy".

North Camberwell has three particularly attractive listed buildings, old almshouses founded by charities as asylums, or what might now be called sheltered housing, for poor elderly people. They are no longer used for this purpose but at least they are all in good use and well restored. The oldest, in Chumleigh Street, a little street leading from Albany Road to Neate Street, are now an oasis, isolated in the expanse of Burgess Park. They are known as Chumleigh Gardens but were erected in 1821 as "The Friendly Female Asylum for aged persons who have seen better days". The small houses around three sides of a garden must have been a pleasant place for old ladies to spend their latter years. With the clearance of the area to make Burgess Park, the almshouses almost fell into ruin, but they have now been beautifully renovated as the headquarters since 1994 of Southwark's Park Rangers Service. The many front doors and windows show that these buildings were once separate houses but it is the young rather than the old who now make use of them. The dividing walls have been demolished to provide longer rooms for games and meetings. The garden is particularly beautiful under the care of the Park Rangers.

Aged Pilgrims Asylum
Completed by voluntary subscriptions, A.D. 1837. For 42 aged pilgrims
The freehold given by William Peacock, Esq. Modernized 1981

This is the inscription above the entrance to what is now called Pilgrim Cloisters, Sedgmoor Place, private flats since 1992. The former residents, or pilgrims, were elderly Christian people of low income, who were provided with these houses by the Aged Pilgrims Society, a charity founded in 1807. The room over the entrance was once their chapel. In the centre of the courtyard garden is a stone marking the burial place of the founder, William Peacock, who died in 1844, aged 89, and also of his wife, Fanny. In Havil Street, backing on to the Aged Pilgrims, is another of Peacock's charitable foundations. The inscription above it once read, "Bethel Asylum for twelve aged women, established A.D.1838 by William Peacock, Esq." These buildings are now council housing.

As the development of North Camberwell continued, the last of the market gardens gave way to streets. Four grand houses were built in Brunswick Park in the 1850s. The pleasant three-storey houses of Vicarage Grove date from the 1860s. Like Brunswick Park they are built on what had earlier been the Glebe, land which provided for the Vicar of St Giles. Benhill Road and Rainbow Street are good examples of North Camberwell's later Victorian streets of two-storey houses. Benhill Road has the simple neat houses of the 1860s, Rainbow Street has all the plaster decoration of flowers and leaves which builders of the 1880s liked even for their most modest houses. But by the time they were built, much of North Camberwell had become a very crowded and poor area.

The Camberwell of Browning and Ruskin

The year's at the spring;
The day's at the morn;
Morning's at seven;
The hill-side's dew-pearled;
The lark's on the wing;
The snail's on the thorn;
God's in his heaven -
All's right with the world!

These lines are from *Pippa Passes,* one of the poems written by Robert Browning when he was living in Camberwell. He and another great writer, John Ruskin, spent their youth in Camberwell at a time when it was still something of a country village, though developing into a suburb of London. North Camberwell is "Browning's Camberwell". The future poet was born in 1812 at Rainbow Cottage, Cottage Green, the most famous person to be actually born in Camberwell. When he was twelve, the family moved to Hanover Cottage, Southampton Way, at what is now the corner of Coleman Road, which was to be his home until 1840. Robert's grandfather had moved to Camberwell in 1784, just the type of professional gentleman who was settling in Camberwell two hundred years ago. He, and later his son, the poet's father, worked at the Bank of England.

Hanover Cottage was a happy home for young Robert and his sister, Sarianna, and here he had an ideal upbringing for a future poet. There was space in North Camberwell, in those days, for a house to have a long back garden with a stable for Robert's pony. His father was a well read man, with a library of 6,000 books and a knowledge of Greek, Latin, French,

Spanish, Italian and Hebrew. When Robert was an old man he remembered how his father taught him about the Siege of Troy.

> My father was a scholar and knew Greek
> When I was five years old, I asked him once
> "What do you read about?"
> "The Siege of Troy"
> "What is a siege and what is Troy?"
> He piled up chairs and tables for a town,
> Set me a-top for Priam, (King of Troy) called our cat
> - Helen, enticed away from home (he said) - -
>
> Robert Browning *Development*

The poem continues with a second cat, two dogs, and a pony, all brought into the story. By the time Robert was twelve he could read about Troy for himself, in the original ancient Greek of Homer's *Iliad*. Robert's mother, Sara, passed on to him her love of animals and nature and also of music. At Hanover Cottage she had a piano, still a fairly rare instrument for a private home. Robert's love of art began with visits to Dulwich Picture Gallery which opened when he was five years old. He said he went there as "a child, far under the age allowed by the regulations - - it used to be a green half-hour's walk over the fields"

From the age of seven to fourteen he was a weekly boarder at Dr Thomas Ready's School in Peckham High Street. After this his studies continued mainly at home with private tutors, including John Relfe, musician to King George III, who lived in Church Row, Camberwell. On Sundays the Browning family attended the York Street Chapel, in what is now Browning Street, Walworth, where Robert and his sister had been baptised. Robert's special companions when he was young were his cousins, James, John and George Silverthorne. Their father owned the old brewery in Peckham Road. James, like Robert, loved art, music and the theatre. One evening, in 1832, Robert walked the ten miles to Richmond to see the famous actor, Edmund Kean, playing Shakespeare's Richard III, "returning on foot through the country lanes in the early morning hours". Robert's other Camberwell friends included some who would later be men of importance. Joseph Arnould, son of a Camberwell doctor, was to become Sir Joseph, a High Court judge in India. Alfred Domett, son of Captain Domett of Camberwell Grove, became Prime Minister of New Zealand. Both are remembered in Camberwell street names.

The one poem by Browning which nearly everyone knows is *The Pied*

Piper of Hamelin. He wrote it in 1842 for the young Willy Macready, whose father was another of Browning's friends, the great actor, William Macready. This was two years after the Browning family had left Camberwell for a larger house in Hatcham, but the poet used an old story

Camberwell, 1842.
From a map of the parish of St Giles, Camberwell by J Dewhirst.

27

that he must have known when he himself was a boy in Camberwell. His father wrote and illustrated another version of it.

> It stood in command of seven acres of healthy ground; - half of it in meadow sloping to the sunrise, the rest divided into - kitchen garden, - orchard - and woodwalk opening to the sunny path by the field. - - And we bought three cows and skimmed our own cream, and churned our own butter. And there was a stable and a farmyard and a haystack and a pigsty.
>
> John Ruskin - *Praeterita*

This is John Ruskin's description of his home from 1842-1872, near the top of Denmark Hill, on its east side. It was here that the great Victorian writer, artist, and thinker wrote most of the books which had so much influence on the thought of his own and later times.

The family had moved out of town in 1823, when John was four, living first at 28 Herne Hill, and then at the larger house, 163 Denmark Hill. Ruskin's father was a partner in a wine-importing firm and, like Browning's father, commuted daily to town. *Praeterita*, Ruskin's autobiography, includes many vivid memories of the Camberwell area. As a small boy he was taken by his nurse to Camberwell Green to see the large pond there, "the sable opacity of its waters adding to the mystery of danger". He was told the fearful story of the wicked boy who had climbed the elm tree beside it on a Sunday, and "had fallen into the pond and - the soul of him into a deeper and darker pool". John Ruskin was mainly educated at home by private tutors, but, when he was fifteen, attended a small private school in Grove Lane kept by the Rev Thomas Dale, Vicar of St Matthew's Church, Denmark Hill (site of King's Dental Hospital). Camberwell Grove, at least, has changed little since those days "a long-drawn aisle, trees, elm, wych elm, sycamore and aspen, the branches meeting at the top; the houses on each side with trim stone pathways up to them, - - three or four storied, mostly in grouped terraces- -" Ruskin had an eye for the type of people who then lived in "their own Grove-world all in all to them", for example, "Mr Gray, having fairly prospered in business and come to London, was established with his wife, her mother and her mother's white French poodle, Petite, in a dignified house in Camberwell Grove". On Sundays the Ruskin family had earlier attended the Beresford Street Chapel, in what is now John Ruskin Street, Walworth. The transition to Denmark Hill had meant "promotion to a distinguished pew in Camden Chapel, quite near the pulpit", to hear the notable preacher, the Rev Henry Melvill. This was in Peckham Road. Ruskin helped to design an extension to the building.

At Denmark Hill, Ruskin entertained the most famous names in Victorian art and literature. He especially admired the works of Turner and acquired many of his water-colours and one oil painting. The breakfast room, he wrote, had "walls mostly covered with lakes by Turner". On 6th February 1843, Ruskin's 24th birthday, Turner visited him at Denmark Hill, "the happiest birthday evening (save one) I ever spent in my life". Other artist friends included Dante Gabriel Rossetti, Sir Edward Burne-Jones and Sir Frederick Leighton. The water-colour artist, Samuel Prout, was a neighbour at 5 De Crespigny Terrace, Denmark Hill. Robert Browning and his wife, Elizabeth Barrett, often came to see Ruskin when they were in London. They were great admirers of his work, and he of theirs. The poet Tennyson, author Charles Kingsley and the American novelist, Henry James, also came to Denmark Hill, and the historian, Thomas Carlyle, rode over from his house in Chelsea. Octavia Hill came, at first to study art, visiting the Dulwich Picture Gallery with Ruskin. Later, it was thanks to him and his generous help from the fortune he inherited from his father, that she was able to begin her life's work as a pioneer in housing reform. His ideas also inspired her when she came to found the National Trust. Ruskin put forward some of his social ideas in his famous lecture on "Work" to the Camberwell Working Men's Institute, at Camberwell Hall, Grove Lane, on 24th January, 1865.

There is not much left in Camberwell now as a reminder of Browning or Ruskin. Rainbow Cottage has gone and the site of Hanover Cottage is a small shop. It has a worn plaque inscribed, "In memory of Robert Browning, born 1812, died 1889, who lived here". There is a sculpture, by Willi Soukup, representing The *Pied Piper*, on the outside wall of the Elmington Estate Community Centre. A later house replaces Ruskin's home on Herne Hill. The house on Denmark Hill survived as a hotel, Ruskin Manor, until it too was demolished in 1949 to build the Denmark Hill housing estate. Ruskin Park across the road, opened in 1907, at least takes the name of Denmark Hill's most famous resident. And Ruskin has left Camberwell one treasure, the East Window of St Giles's Church, designed by him and Edmund Oldfield, his old school friend from the Grove Lane school. There are drawings by Ruskin in the permanent collection at the South London Gallery and books by him, and from his old home, in the Local Studies Library.

3. PART OF THE GREAT METROPOLIS

Transport by road and rail

In the early days, horse power was the only means of transport for commuters from Camberwell. By about 1800 two firms each ran coaches seven times a day from Camberwell to Gracechurch Street in the City. There was also a hackney carriage stand outside the Father Redcap, rather like a taxi rank today. But coach and carriage fares were quite high. The journey was also slow, made the more so by the tollgate across the Walworth Road, near Walworth Common, now Westmoreland Road. A Turnpike Trust had taken over the old highway from the Elephant and Castle to Camberwell Green in 1782 and was allowed to collect tolls for the upkeep of the road. Only the well-paid, and those who did not have to work long hours, could as yet live out of town in this pleasant suburb.

In the 1830s a new type of horse transport which could carry more people appeared on the roads; the horse-bus. In 1851 Thomas Tilling set up his own horse-bus business in Peckham High Street. His first buses carried people from Camberwell to the Great Exhibition held that year in Hyde Park. They travelled from Peckham, via Camberwell Green, on the route still used by the 12 bus. Within a few years a regular and frequent bus service got going and there were buses to and from Camberwell crossing London, Blackfriars, Waterloo and Westminster Bridge every five minutes. Tilling's buses were so successful that his firm eventually became one of the foundations of London Transport.

In 1862 trains came to Camberwell, the first public transport that was not horse-drawn. The people who lived in the terrace houses of Camberwell New Road must have been particularly aware of the sight and sound of noisy steam engines puffing out smoke as they travelled across the railway bridge, high above the horse drawn traffic below. The line from Herne Hill, run by the London Chatham and Dover Railway Company (the LCDR), had a station in what is still called Station Road, and another, known as Camberwell Gate, or Walworth Road, half way to the Elephant and Castle, in John Ruskin Street. In 1868 the South London and Sutton

Railway opened Champion Hill, now East Dulwich Station. All local residents were now within walking distance of a station; but the most central station for most of them was, and still is, Denmark Hill, opened in 1866 by the London Brighton and South Coast Railway (the LBSCR).

Only the names of pubs, the Station Hotel at the corner of Station Road, and the Station Tavern in John Ruskin Street, are reminders of the Camberwell New Road and the Camberwell Gate stations, which both closed in 1916. Denmark Hill, however, is still very much in use, and the fine station building has had a new lease of life. Victorian station builders often imitated styles of architecture used for elegant buildings of earlier times. Denmark Hill has been described as "a Tuscan villa in the heart of Camberwell" with domed roofs at either side which are said to be "in French style". Once there was a large waiting room with mahogany seats and open fires and two ticket offices for the two companies which used it, the LBSCR and the LCDR. The station master wore a black frock coat with gold braid and a peaked hat with his title proudly on it in gold letters. He and his family lived in the north block of the station. By the 1980's however such a large station was no longer needed, it had also been set on fire by vandals. It was saved from demolition, thanks largely to a campaign led by the Camberwell Society, and superbly restored, winning a Civic Trust Award in 1986. There is now a smaller booking office and the remainder of the building is converted into a pub, the Phoenix and Firkin. Like the phoenix, a mythical bird, it has risen again from the flames.

Peckham Road, c. 1905
Looking west from the junction with Southhampton Way.

The coming of the trains made a great difference for poorer people. Workers on long hours and low wages now had a quick, cheap, means of transport. In the early years there were Workmen's Tickets, at a penny each way, for those who travelled before 7.00 am and returned after 6.00 pm. For the first time such people could live farther from their work than just their legs could carry them.

Soon after the first trains, another new cheap form of transport appeared, this time on the main Camberwell roads. Tramlines were laid and by 1871 double-decker trams were running from the Elephant and Castle to Camberwell Green and, soon after, along Peckham Road to New Cross, and along Coldharbour Lane to Brixton. These early trams were horse - powered but, with the help of rails, two horses could draw a much heavier load than the old horse-buses. Fares were therefore lower, and on the trams too workmen benefitted from cheap early morning travel. The change from horse to electric trams began in 1903 when the London County Council took over the tramways. These were still cheaper, and carried more passengers, than the motor buses which came in soon after. In 1908 the service was extended via Denmark Hill and Champion Park to Dog Kennel Hill and hence to Peckham Rye and Dulwich.

Most trams were powered by electric cable laid under the tramlines. Those going to Brixton, however, got their power from overhead wires. A change pit at the Camberwell end of Coldharbour Lane enabled trams to change from one to the other. There was a tramway depot between Camberwell Road and Camberwell New Road, later rebuilt as a bus garage, but closed in 1985. Camberwell Green was an exceptionally busy junction for trams. At peak times as many as 250 trams, on 14 different routes, passed there every hour. The author, Richard Church, when young, travelled daily from his home on Herne Hill to his work in town. He described the scene at Camberwell Green in his autobiography, *The Golden Sovereign,*

> The constant movement of the brown monsters, giants with neither head nor tail - -the interweaving of these trams, impervious to the - - traffic that rushed, dodged and cut in around them, mounted during rush hours to a nightmare fantasy. The roar of it, the clangour of the gongs, the sudden formations in a halted procession of these land-arks; the surge forward, the partings, with shrieks of vehicular agony at rail-points; - - the menace of the road surfaces, - - its armoury of razor-edged rails; all these things, a piling up of threats and horrors, came to a sinister perfection at Camberwell Green.

Trams came to an end throughout London in 1952. Despite their disadvantages many people remember them with affection and some praise them as an energy-saving form of transport that may well return.

Various efforts have been made over the years to bring the Underground to Camberwell, but so far it has not come nearer than the Oval and the Elephant and Castle. Meanwhile, those travelling on two wheels are well served by Edwardes cycle shop, in Camberwell Road since 1910, though founded earlier by an all England cycling champion. Such celebrities as Sterling Moss and Laurence Olivier have shopped there and the firm is proud of its Royal Warrant, awarded in 1972, for supplying, at that time, mopeds for Buckingham Palace messengers.

Victorian Suburb

Victorian Suburb was the title that H J Dyos, Professor of Urban History at Leicester University, gave to his important book on the growth of Camberwell. It was during the long reign of Queen Victoria (1837-1901) that Camberwell completely changed from something of a village into a part of the inner-city. As Blanch wrote in 1875, "From a straggling suburban parish of about 4,000 inhabitants, Camberwell has become a congeries of streets, part of the great metropolis itself. Bricks and mortar, and universal stucco, have invaded the place-". How was it that such changes occurred? Well, firstly the population of London increased, engulfing all the surrounding villages. Secondly, central London's businesses, factories, warehouses, and especially railways, left less room there for people to live . Thirdly and, most importantly, there was now cheap, quick, public transport for the masses. As may easily be seen from maps and from population figures, the greatest changes to Camberwell came just after the coming of the railways and the trams. In 1801 there were 7,059 people living in the Parish of Camberwell (Camberwell, Peckham and Dulwich). By 1841, the first census of Queen Victoria's reign, there were 39,868; by 1901, there were 259,339, far more than now live in the whole of the London Borough of Southwark. But the biggest increase was in the thirty years, 1861-1891. In 1861 the population figure was 71,488. In 1891 it was 235,344.

As the area became more crowded the class of people living here also changed. Poor people moved in and the wealthy moved out to more spacious and peaceful places. John Ruskin, for example, left Denmark Hill for the

Lake District soon after the railway came. The Georgian houses on Camberwell Road were no longer each the home of a single family but now had many occupants and shops were built in their front gardens; in fact the road, by 1892, was "noted as one of the best and cheapest shopping thoroughfares in London".

Many people in Camberwell are still living in a Victorian suburb. Much of the street plan was laid out in the later years of Queen Victoria's reign, and many of the houses were built then, if not earlier. Their owners like them. They were soundly built. The best late Victorian streets are mostly south of Peckham Road. From the type of houses it is easy to see that the first people who lived in them were fairly prosperous middle class families. They were not the kind who had to take in lodgers to make ends meet, as was done in poorer streets. They liked to keep up appearances. *In the year of Jubilee* is a novel set in 1887, the year of Queen Victoria's Golden Jubilee. It pictures a Mr Peachey living in a house in De Crespigny Park, which might be one of those still there today, with its flight of steps to the stucco pillars at the entrance. According to the author, George Gissing, "De Crespigny Park in point of respectability, has claims only to be appreciated by the ambitious middle class of Camberwell. Each house seems to remind its neighbour, with all the complacence expressible in buff brick, that in this locality lodgings are not to let". But even so, there was no room now in Camberwell for grand mansions with large grounds. De Crespigny Park was one of the streets built on the De Crespigny estate. The whole of Bushey Hill Road with over 200 houses was built on another estate, the residence in 1820 of an Admiral, Sir John Knight. The roads between Wilson Road and Vestry Road were built by a Mr Purkis on what had been the grounds of the old Wilson's Grammar School. They were named after three members of his family, Grace, Maude and Dagmar. The fields between Camberwell Grove and Lyndhurst Road, Peckham, which had never been built on, disappeared at this time.

Shops and businesses around Camberwell Green catered well for the early residents of the better class houses. One firm, which could have had such houses on its books when they were new, is still in business. Alexander Robertson set himself up in 1884 as an estate agent and auctioneer. In 1989, still in the Robertson family, the firm merged with an even older family firm, W Andrew and Son, of 75 Camberwell Church Street, to become Andrews & Robertson, at Robertson's office, 27 Camberwell Green, a house built in 1836. Wickes, the undertakers, are also still in business. They have been in Camberwell since 1847 and on Denmark Hill since 1870. For the funerals of Victorian residents they used to provide "a large number of well appointed funeral carriages and a stud of suitable horses".

Russell's, 64-75 Denmark Hill, was "a ladies outfitters of a very high standard", according to a lady who remembered it. The building, minus a top storey which it lost in World War II, is now a Nat West Bank. The grand, but rather run-down, buildings at the corner of Denmark Hill and Camberwell New Road, were once Horsley's, "a good class grocer's". The landmark of Camberwell Green, the impressive building with a tower, rather like a Victorian Town Hall, on the north corner of Camberwell New

George Waller's, complete outfitters, 27 - 31 Camberwell Church St, c. 1900.

Road, was erected in 1899 as the London & County Bank, later Nat West, which occupied it until 1993. The former Barclays Bank at the corner of Wren Road and Camberwell Church Street is another good Victorian building. 14 Camberwell Church Street, now a sports shop, was once Gibberd's shoe shop where, according to the founder's great grandson, Graham Gibberd, "shoes were measured to fit, with wooden lasts made of the feet of the customers, and hung in rows on the wall".

The curving north side of Camberwell Church Street is all part of one Victorian redevelopment undertaken in the 1880s when the road was widened for the trams. It is unchanged above the modern shop fronts. 27-31 were originally Wallers, a gentlemen's outfitters, and what is now the Dome Hotel was J Mackie & co., drapers. Hidden behind the shops, with an entrance from Artichoke Place, is Artichoke Mews, erected in 1887, as a stable block, when horse drawn vans would have delivered goods to the shops. It has been well restored, by the Southwark Environment Trust, for flats, workshops and offices.

Crowded streets

Camberwell, north of Peckham Road, was very different. This was the industrial area of the Victorian Suburb. Old maps show it, before World War II, as a maze of small streets and factories. According to Blanch, St George's Church, in 1875, "now stands among houses packed in those close rows, which almost seem to keep out the free air of heaven from their inhabitants". Along the Canal banks, factories made linoleum, paints, jam, beer, etc. Before fridges came into use there was even an ice warehouse. Watkin's "Bible Factory" which bound a million bibles a year for the British and Foreign Bible Society and employed 400 people, was hemmed in between four little streets, all now completely gone, in the middle of what is now Burgess Park. At one time there were at least four mineral water works near the canal. Horses and carts carrying the rattling bottles of drink over cobbled streets were a familiar sound. The best known firm was R White and Co., a name which still appears on bottles of fizzy lemonade, but it is no longer made in Camberwell. Another famous firm was Samuel Jones, established in Camberwell in 1868. It chose the Camberwell Beauty butterfly as its trademark to show how it could print

"The Bible Factory", Watkins & Co., bookbinders, Cowan St, c. 1930.

colour on its gummed paper. Butterfly Brand sticky tape was another of the firm's special products, a forerunner of sellotape. The huge sign of a butterfly, made of ceramic tiles, was a well known sight above the firm's 1920's factory at the junction of Southampton Way and Peckham Grove. When Samuel Jones moved out of Camberwell and the factory was demolished the sign was re-erected on the outside of the old Baths building in Wells Way. The butterfly from the firm's other premises in Orpheus Street is now on the outside of the Butterfly Walk Shopping Centre, Denmark Hill.

As well as large factories, North Camberwell had many small workshops. Some of the older houses in Parkhouse Street, once just family homes, were taken over by laundries which used their long back gardens for hanging out the clothes - very useful in the days before washing machines and spin dryers. As a reminder of the past, the chimney from one laundry has been left standing in the new Industrial Estate. The Hunnexes, producers of cartons and packaging, are one family firm still operating and living at

35 Parkhouse Street, where they have been since 1913, though fork-lift trucks have replaced the horses of their founder, Jonathan Hunnex. They were pioneers of recycling before the idea had been invented, building up a business by turning inside out and relabelling old surplus cardboard boxes. At 41, before World War II, was a Georgian villa, the home and also the engineering works of the Wyard family. The scent of roasting nuts from Whiteside's Sun Pat factory hung over Parkhouse Street at that period. Today the street is largely rebuilt with modern industries. Others are part of the Camberwell Business Centre, Lomond Grove.

The people who lived in North Camberwell were mostly working class. They liked the friendliness of their little back streets, and their houses with backyards where they could keep a few rabbits or chickens. They had no grand stores, but little shops; for example, Ethel Neate's, in Dalwood Street, "an ideal place for a penn'orth of this or that if you ran a bit short towards the end of the week". Mr Fulljames, who was brought up in the street, recalled how "we used to gallop round there for "a penn'orth of mustard pickles please", in a cup with no handle". The children had nowhere to play but the streets, but before motor traffic these were fairly safe. They also had the canal for fishing and, though it was dirty and dangerous, even for swimming.

There was however a much darker side to the Victorian Suburb. "The poor, squeezed out of other parts come here and Camberwell suffers" said the Chairman of Camberwell Vestry in 1890. As more and more people from inner London crowded into North Camberwell some parts became so densely populated and so poor that they were nothing more than slums. Every inch of land was needed and houses were even built in the back gardens of other houses,what Dyos ironically called "a garden suburb of an unusual kind". Sometimes, as many as six houses might be built on a plot intended for just one house. One black spot was a confusion of alleys and courtyards between Camberwell Road, Camberwell Green and Lomond Grove; where only about twenty years before there had been market gardens. An even worse area was a block of streets west of Camberwell Road, between Crown Street, Wyndham Road and Bethwin Road. They were almost sealed off from the main road by the railway arches. Charles Booth, in his great survey, *Labour and life of the people in London* described Sultan Street in 1889 as "one of the vilest slums in the whole of London". Children, often without shoes, filled the streets. Houses were terribly overcrowded, for example, 21 Hollington Street, a three-storey house of six rooms was home to nineteen people, including eleven children. The mother on the ground floor did not send her three children to school, "because they are so ragged". The top back room was occupied by four children with their father, "who drinks what he gets". Anyone straying into this area from the more refined parts of Camberwell would have been hit firstly by the smell. It came from the piggeries and cowsheds, which were still there among the houses, from glue and linoleum factories, and from haddock being smoked in back yards. In addition, every bit of space was used for stabling ponies and donkeys and storing market barrows. The rotting vegetable rubbish from these added to the sickly atmosphere.

The worst slum areas were eventually cleared by the London County Council and are now covered by council housing. Before this some other attempts had already been made to provide better housing for the poorest people. George Peabody, a rich American businessman, who had seen the conditions in parts of London, had given a large sum of money for this purpose back in 1862. The flats on Camberwell Green, erected in 1910, are one of the estates built by the Peabody Trust. Evelina Mansions in New Church Road, erected in 1900 by the Four Percent Industrial Dwellings Company, and the Samuel Lewis Trust Buildings, Warner Road, of 1915, are similar developments. Although these were all dwellings for the poor they were well built in the grand style. Now that they have been renovated, and modernised inside, they make comfortable flats for people of today.

For the very poorest of the poor of the Victorian Suburb, there was just one last refuge, the big workhouse in Havil Street. It had replaced the earlier small building on Peckham Road in 1815 and later had been much enlarged. In 1874, 422 people were reduced to living there and 107 in the infirmary attached to it. Able-bodied male paupers were marched daily to a stone-yard by the canal to earn their keep by breaking up stones. Earlier, poor children, like Oliver Twist, had also been brought up in the workhouse, but since 1855 these had been sent away from their parents (if they had any) to the Poor Law District Schools at Sutton in Surrey. 371 Camberwell children were boarded there in 1874. Very poor families who were "on the parish" but just managed to stay in their own homes, went weekly to Havil Street to collect their dole or outdoor relief. This was given to them not in money, to buy what they liked, but in rations, and loaves of bread.

4. IMPORTANT BUILDINGS

Churches and chapels

St Giles, Peckham Road, the parish church of Camberwell, was built in 1844. It is much larger than the old church which it replaced and is, in fact, one of the larger parish churches of England. It was designed by the architect, Sir George Gilbert Scott, and was his first important building in the Gothic style, the style that is, of churches of the Middle Ages, with tall pointed arches and windows. He was later to become famous as the leading architect of the Gothic Revival in England. All over the country there are churches built or restored by him. In London, however, perhaps he is best known as the architect of St Pancras Station and the Albert Memorial. When St Giles was damaged in World War II, it was restored by another important church architect, Sir Ninian Comper. Now it is again being restored, with support from English Heritage and the European Union, as an important work of architecture.

The special glory of St Giles is its beautiful east window. From the nave it looks just a mosaic of bright colours. Seen more closely, from the chancel, it reveals pictures of many Bible stories. In the centre are scenes from the life of Christ. On the left are Old Testament scenes. The rainbow from the story of Noah's Ark, and Jacob's Ladder, are easy to find. The window is famous as the only surviving stained glass by John Ruskin. He said it was designed mainly by his friend, Edmund Oldfield, but Ruskin visited the great French cathedrals, Chartres and Rouen, especially to get ideas for it and copied their rich colours. The stained glass in the West window of St Giles is about 700 years old and came from Trier in Germany. It was given by the Reverend George Storie, vicar when the church was being built. The windows in the south transept are by Sir Ninian Comper. Another special feature of St Giles is its Bishop organ, made by J C Bishop, founder of a firm of organ builders. It was designed by Samuel Sebastian Wesley, the eminent organist, who had been organist at the old St Giles. The church also has a fine peal of bells in the tower, and has a team of bell ringers.

The modern St George's, the parish church of North Camberwell, is part of the Trinity College Centre, Coleman Road. The congregation moved

St Giles's Church, c. 1850
From a water-colour by W Waller at the South London Gallery.

there in 1982, though the connection with the College goes back to 1885
when North Camberwell was a poor and crowded area, and Trinity College,
Cambridge, took over the care of the parish. The old St George's Church
in Wells Way is one of Camberwell's finest buildings and now looks, from
the outside, almost as it did when new in 1824. It was a Waterloo Church,
one of the churches erected soon after the Battle of Waterloo ended the

long wars against Napoleon. Sometimes they are known as Commissioners' Churches as they were built with help from the Church Building Commissioners, set up to provide new churches in areas where population had increased. The architect was Francis Bedford who lived for a time in Camberwell Grove. Like his other churches, St John's, Waterloo, St Luke's, Norwood and Holy Trinity, Trinity Church Square, it is in the classical style, similar to the temples of ancient Greece. By 1970, however, the little streets around it had gone. The church was almost surrounded by open space. The roof needed a large sum for repairs. It was abandoned and for over twenty years stood almost in ruins. Happily, in 1993, mainly thanks to a local campaign to save it, the old church was beautifully restored and converted to new use. Within its walls, thirty one-bedroom housing society flats have been built around the roofless nave. Only the newly gilded cross on the tower still serves as a reminder of the building's original purpose.

Love Walk United Reformed Church is a plain-looking building, erected in 1960. It gives no clue to the long history of this church, which began in 1774 when a group of Dissenters, or non-conformist Christians, began meeting at the old Bowyer Mansion House, Camberwell Road. Samuel Favell, a deacon at the Mansion House Chapel, was a famous supporter of religious and civil liberty and helped to put an end to slavery in countries under British rule. In 1853 the church moved to a fine new Gothic building at the south end of Wren Road, the site earlier of "the old house on the Green". It became Camberwell Green, or Wren Road, Congregational Church. In 1960 the congregation sold this building for redevelopment and with the proceeds built their Love Walk church, which has plenty of room both for worship and for community activities.

Grove Chapel, Camberwell Grove, erected in 1819, is the oldest place of worship in Camberwell still meeting in its original building. The architect was David Roper who also designed St Mark's Church near the Oval. The interior of this Independent Chapel is beautiful with a fine pulpit made by Joseph Irons, its founder and first minister. When young he had trained as a carpenter. The sermons he preached from this pulpit were published and widely read. Denmark Place Baptist Church, Coldharbour Lane, has a history going back to 1802 and has been in its present building since 1825. Comber Grove is named after Thomas Comber, born nearby in Councillor Street, who was a member of this church. He and other members of his family gave their lives as missionaries in Africa, where he died in 1887.

Cottage Green Baptist Chapel has survived all the changes in North Camberwell since at least 1840. The part facing Wells Way, rebuilt in 1972, is now the church. The old building in Cottage Green provides offices for Pecan, an imaginative project, run by evangelical churches, to combat unemployment on the north Peckham estates. The South London Baptist Tabernacle, founded in 1880, now meets in Welton Hall, Bushey Hill Road. Welton Court, sheltered housing for the elderly, is built on the site of the original Victorian church in Peckham Road.

The noticeboard outside a church in Camberwell New Road is in Greek as well as in English. Since 1963 this has been St Mary's Greek Orthodox Cathedral. Inside, the screen, or iconostasis, at the east end, is covered with icons, glittering with gold paint, pictures of Christ and the saints in the Greek Orthodox style. The building itself was erected in 1876 for a very different congregation. They were members of the Catholic Apostolic Church, a sect which has almost disappeared. The architect was John Belcher, a member of the church, who lived at Redholm, Champion Hill, which he also designed. The house stands next to the later buildings of the Fox on the Hill. Calvary Temple, at the corner of Councillor Street and Camberwell New Road, another interesting building, has an Italian style tower and belfry. This church was built in 1891 for the Baptists who moved in 1975 to the new Brandon Baptist Church, Redcar Street.

Several other churches have modern buildings but a longer history. Old photographs looking south from Camberwell Green show the spire of St Matthew's Church, Denmark Hill, standing out above the rooftops. Destroyed in World War II, it was replaced by St Matthew's, Lilford Road. St Michael's, Wyndham Road, is a very small but eye-catching building with its miniature spire of coloured glass. It was erected as part of the Archbishop Michael Ramsey School development, to replace two Victorian churches, St Michael's, Sultan Street and All Souls, Grosvenor Park. In 1994 it had the distinction of having the first woman vicar in London. The first Roman Catholic church in Camberwell, opened in 1860, was destroyed in the war. The new Sacred Heart Church, Camberwell New Road, opened in 1953. The Camberwell Evangelical Church, Bethwin Road, is a small building, more like a tenants' hall, but doing good work in this uninspiring area of Council estates.

The 1913 *Ordnance Survey Map* shows that, no one living in the crowded streets of North Camberwell was far from some church, chapel, or mission hall. St George's, in addition to the church in Wells Way, had mission halls in Albany Road, New Church Road and St George's Road. These, like other churches and missions, were centres, not just for Sunday worship and huge Sunday Schools for the children, but also for many weekday community activities and help for the very poor such as soup kitchens and free breakfasts. Most were swept away without trace after World War II, together with the streets they served. One of the longest lived was the Zion Methodist Church, Neate Street, 1855-1964.

Two historic Camberwell churches have also gone. Ruskin's Camden Church was destroyed in the war; Sceaux Gardens flats cover the site. Emmanuel Church, Camberwell Road, was also replaced by flats, Churchmead and Bishopsmead. Emmanuel was probably the church Dickens had in mind in his novel, *Great Expectations*, "We went towards Camberwell Green, and - - Wemmick said suddenly 'Halloa! Here's a church. - - We went in, Wemmick leaving his fishing rod in the porch, and looked all round. 'Halloa' said Wemmick, 'Here's Miss Skiffins! Let's have a wedding"

Schools old and new

The oldest school buildings still standing in Camberwell are now an extension to the Town Hall, Peckham Road. Two hundred years ago what is now known as East House was Alfred House, or Dr Wanostrocht's Academy, one of several schools in Camberwell and Peckham educating the sons and daughters of well-off families. Dr Nicolas Wanostrocht, a Belgian, opened his school in 1795. He wrote books on French, Latin, and English grammar and other school subjects, and no doubt parents of the forty boys sent here as boarders were impressed with such a learned schoolmaster. They also appreciated the school's healthy country setting. Every week there were rambles in the fields near the school for nature study. Day boys would have come from some of Camberwell's Georgian houses. Cricket lovers have special reason to remember the school's third headmaster, Dr Wanostrocht's great nephew, known as Nicholas Felix, a great cricketer, and author of *Felix on the Bat*, the first book of cricket rules and instructions, which had world-wide influence. Nicholas had first played cricket at Harry Hampton's Ground, Cottage Green, and his first appearance at Lords was in a Camberwell XI against Uxbridge. In 1832 when Alfred House School moved to Blackheath, the old building was occupied by the Royal Naval School until this too moved out, to what is now Goldsmiths' College, Lewisham Way. From 1846 to 1954, the school buildings housed the Camberwell House Asylum, for the mentally ill. Sceaux Gardens Estate was built in the grounds of Camberwell House.

Some of Camberwell's grand mansions also became, for a time, schools for young gentlemen, for example, the Bowyer Mansion House Academy. From 1837 to 1873, Denmark Hill Grammar School occupied an old house on Denmark Hill dating back at least to 1656. Boys at this school, under its first headmaster, Joseph Payne, were certainly fortunate. His books on education put forward such modern ideas as that classrooms should be places of "learning and not lecturing" and that corporal punishment was unnecessary in a well managed school. Shops now cover the site of the school and the Selbourne estate its old grounds, which stretched from Love Walk to Daneville Road. From 1840, until it was demolished, Dr Lettsom's Villa was a girls' school, Pelican House, conducted by the Misses McDowall of Grove Park. Camberwell Collegiate School for Boys on the east side of Camberwell Grove, opposite the Grove Chapel, was rather different, being purpose-built in 1834 in the style of an Oxford or Cambridge College. Soon however the character of Camberwell began changing. As with most others of its kind, by 1867 the school was demolished and its land used for building.

In the past many children whose parents could not afford school fees had no schooling at all. Some were able to go to charity or church schools such as the Greencoat School. The Mansion House Chapel was especially concerned with the poorest of the poor, and there were some of these in the back streets even of genteel Georgian Camberwell. About 1810, members of the Chapel opened a Free School in Nelson Street (now Toulon Street), off Bowyer Lane, now Wyndham Road, a street described in an early school report as, "proverbial for its depravity as for its ignorance". The school was supported by pioneers in the education of the poor such as Samuel Favell, and by James Wilson, of Denmark Hill, who had been captain of the first ship sent out by the London Missionary Society. The portico with columns, now in Ruskin Park, was once part of his house. The school later became a British School, supported by the British and Foreign Bible Society, and moved to Comber Grove. Nelson Street became a Ragged School, for the very poorest. It was a member of the Ragged Schools Union. The teachers were mostly unpaid volunteers. They faced many difficult tasks, coping not only with ragged, unwashed urchins all day but also with mud-slinging, jeering yobs as they trudged to and from school.

St George's Church of England Primary School, Coleman Road, built in 1964, is the school with the longest history still going strong in Camberwell. It was founded by St George's Church in 1826 for children from the new streets of North Camberwell. Like other church schools it became a National School, helped by the National Society for promoting the education of the poor. Fred Nichols, a teacher at the school in the 1930s, recalled that even in his time there were some children so poor they had no shoes to come to school. But he also remembered the school treats. In 1935, the year of King George V's Silver Jubilee, the children had visits to the Crystal Palace and to the Coronet cinema in Wells Way. The old school building was destroyed in World War II. Archbishop Michael Ramsey, the Church of England Secondary School in Farmers Road, was erected in 1974 and is named after the Archbishop of Canterbury at that time. It too has links with the past as it was built with the funds of thirteen much older schools in Lambeth and Southwark. It even has the figure of a Charity School boy, dated 1785, which came from one of them. The schools included St Mary Newington, founded in 1710, which was on the site of the Elephant and Castle Leisure Centre, and St Michael and All Angels School which was in Sultan Street. There are two Roman Catholic Schools in Camberwell, St Joseph's Primary School, Pitman Street, built in 1904, and the Sacred Heart Secondary School, Camberwell New Road, rebuilt in 1959.

In 1870 the government decided to make education compulsory for all children. The Education Act set up School Boards to provide sufficient schools. Inspectors found that there were only about 7,000 places in free schools in Camberwell, Peckham and Dulwich but over 23,000 children were needing them. Many Board Schools were built in the next few years by the School Board for London. Comber Grove is one of the oldest, built in 1877, replacing the old British School. Crawford also traces its history back to a British School, founded in 1841, which was taken over and rebuilt. At one time Crawford was a Higher Grade or Central School where children had a more advanced education, something between an ordinary elementary school and a secondary school. Since 1940 it has been just a junior and infants school. Many former Board Schools have a plaque high up on the outside giving their original name and date. The plaque on Oliver Goldsmith School reads "L S B Peckham Road School 1899". It was renamed after the famous 18th century writer who was once a teacher in Peckham. Oliver Goldsmith is now a primary school but, like most Board schools, was built on a three floored plan to take all ages up to fourteen, school leaving age. James Fulljames, who started at Oliver Goldsmith in 1912, remembered

> "There were three floors. Ground floor was infants, middle floor girls, and top floor boys. I, like all the other kids I knew, started school when I was four. - - At the age of eight we really started to live and moved upstairs into the boys' school. There were six classes, ranging from class two to class seven. Seven really, part of seven was called 'ex-seven'".

The plaque on the outside of Lyndhurst School, Grove Lane, reads "LCC Denmark Hill Schools 1905". The London County Council took over from the London School Board in 1904. The crowded streets of North Camberwell must have been full of children and huge schools were built for them. Brunswick Park, partly rebuilt in 1961, and Cobourg, are still in use, though now only as primary schools. The Southampton Street (Way) Schools are now the Camberwell Centre for Southwark College. Albany Road School, built in 1877, had so many pupils by 1904 that it had to be enlarged. Like most schools it has separate entrances, inscribed boys, girls, and infants, and a bell turret where the bell once summoned them to lessons, but it is no longer needed as a school. It is used as an annexe to the Southwark Education Department. Southwark schools passed from the LCC to the Inner London Education Authority in 1965 and to Southwark Borough Council in 1990.

Two important buildings which provided some of the best education for Camberwell boys and girls until fairly recent years are no longer schools, though used for other good purposes. One was the historic Wilson's Grammar School rebuilt in 1882 to designs by E R Robson, Architect of the London School Board. Famous old Wilsonians included Walter Matthews who became Dean of St Paul's, Sir James Jeans, mathematician and astronomer, and Sir Alan Cobham, pioneer airman. Mary Datchelor School for Girls, Camberwell Grove, opened in 1876. The movement to give women equality with men was beginning and the aim of this school was to give the daughters of middle class families as good an education as their sons. It was named after Mary Datchelor who, in 1726, with her sisters, had given their estate to help poor children of their parish in the City. 150 years later the charity was put to new use to found this school. In their later years both Wilson's and Mary Datchelor charged no fees but took all their pupils from those who had passed the Eleven Plus examination. When comprehensive schools came in both these grammar schools decided they could no longer continue in Camberwell. In 1975 Wilson's moved out to Sutton. Its Camberwell buildings are now the Wilson Annexe to the Camberwell College of Art. Before Wilson's moved out, it used the funds of the old Greencoat School to build the Greencoat Building, Wilson Road, now the South London Science and Technology Centre. Since 1982 the Mary Datchelor building has been the headquarters of the Save the Children Fund.

Public buildings

The Town Hall, Peckham Road, is now the headquarters of Southwark's local government. In 1965 three metropolitan boroughs, Bermondsey, Camberwell and Southwark were amalgamated to form the new London Borough of Southwark, stretching from the River Thames in the north to Sydenham Hill in the south. What had been the Camberwell Town Hall was chosen to be the Town Hall for the new Southwark. In fact, this part of Camberwell had long been the site of local government. In 1827, as Camberwell developed, the Vestry found their work increasing, and built their first Vestry Hall, on the opposite corner of Havil Street from the present Town Hall. A much larger Vestry Hall was erected across the road in 1873 and, in 1900, when Camberwell became a Metropolitan Borough, this became the Camberwell Town Hall. The Mayor and Council of Southwark now meet in the Council Chamber of that building, but most of the Town Hall was rebuilt in 1934.

"Do Today's Work Today" is the motto above the offices across Havil Street from the Town Hall, erected in 1904, on the site of the first Vestry Hall. The first people to read this motto on their way to work were the Camberwell Board of Guardians and their staff. Before there was any Department of Social Security, it was the duty of this local committee to assist the very poor and unemployed, visiting them first to make sure only the really destitute got any help. In *Times of our Lives*, Alf Slater, born in Sultan Street in 1927, one of a large family, recalled the weekly visit to his widowed mother, "by the man from the Guardians, with his charitable pittance, quizzing eyes and prying information". Before the National Health Service the guardians were also responsible for St Giles Hospital, three institutions or workhouses in Havil Street, Gordon Road and St Francis

Road, and for homes for poor children. In 1930 their duties passed to the London County Council and in 1948 the hospital passed to the NHS. Their building is now an extension to the Town Hall.

In Wells Way, amid all the open space and modern housing stands a grand, ornate building, erected in 1902. The architect was Maurice Adams. It is a mixture of old styles of architecture, described as a "picturesque group with Baroque porch, Gothic gable, Tudor windows, and a Queen Anne bay window". Part of the building, now premises of the Southwark Groundwork Trust, was, until 1991, the North Camberwell Public Library. The other part, now used for boxing, was the North Camberwell Public Baths and Washhouses, much appreciated, when it was first opened, by people living nearby in houses with no bathrooms, washing machines or constant hot water. As Stan Hall recalled in *Times of our Lives,*

> We had baths in Wells Way, quite close to our home. For three pence you were supplied with a small square of soap and what appeared to be a length of corrugated paper (they said it was a towel) - Inside you were in a large space with cubicles of black stone, open topped. The attendant would lead you to one. Inside was a large bath of the same colour. The attendant would turn on a tap outside and a flow of water would enter the bath. - - Shouts could be heard for 'A drop more hot for No.6' or 'More cold in No.13', as well as curses should cold be turned on where hot was wanted - - Under the Baths was the Wash-house, where mothers could bring their weekly wash; for a penny or tuppence they had use of a sink and hot water, also a wringer to remove most of the water before taking it back home to dry.

The Camberwell Leisure Centre in Artichoke Place, Camberwell Church Street, is a Victorian building which has been splendidly restored to its original appearance, as it was when it was proudly opened by the Camberwell Vestry in 1891. It was then the Camberwell Baths, and the swimming bath is still much in use. Many other activities now also take place at the Centre, such as table tennis, badminton and gymnastics. Nearby is Camberwell Library, now the only library in the Camberwell neighbourhood. It opened in 1944, during World War II, as a partial replacement for the fine old Central Library on the south side of Peckham Road, which had been destroyed by bombing. The Church Street library is so popular that it has recently been extended, taking over another shop.

In Havil Street, nearly opposite the Town Hall, there is a very unusual round tower in cream coloured brickwork, five storeys high. This is St Giles's Tower, now converted into eighteen private flats. It was built, in

1888, for quite a different purpose. It was a ward block of St Giles's Hospital specially designed in accordance with the medical ideas of the time. The hospital itself, Camberwell's oldest, had begun much earlier as an infirmary for poor people, attached to the Camberwell Workhouse. Designers of the round block, knowing nothing of bacteria or viruses, believed that disease was spread by miasmas which came from sick people. In a round ward, it was thought, patients would get as much fresh air and sunlight as possible and be kept away from each other. If well enough, they could also sit out on the balconies. Only a few such towers were built and St Giles is a rare survival, preserved and restored thanks to a campaign by the Camberwell and Peckham Societies, the Victorian Society and local residents. The hospital itself once stretched from St Giles Road to Havil Street, and had beds, in the 1930s, for 800 patients, and its own nurses' training school. It mainly closed in 1984 when its services were transferred to King's College Hospital. Most of it was demolished and new private housing, Gables Close, was built on the site. The Administration Block in St Giles Road, still used for health service purposes, was erected in 1904 in the Arts and Crafts style of architecture. It is now, like St Giles Tower, a listed building.

Denmark Hill is famed far and wide for its two great teaching hospitals. The Maudsley was erected in 1914 and named after Henry Maudsley, an eminent psychiatrist and professor at University College, London, who gave £30,000 towards its foundation. The hospital has been a pioneer in the treatment of mental and neurological illness. Its Institute of Psychiatry has trained most of the professors of psychiatry in this country. The Maudsley is now amalgamated with the Royal Bethlem Hospital, a much older foundation. King's College Hospital, one of London's largest hospitals, is just in Lambeth but is the headquarters for the Camberwell health authority, King's Health Care. The hospital, founded in 1840 near the Strand, moved to Denmark Hill in 1913. Its School of Medicine and Dentistry is part of King's College, London University. The Camberwell Green Health Centre, opened in 1994, is the most modern health-care building in Camberwell. Its imaginative design, with large south facing windows, is the work of well-known local architects, John and Selina Eger.

Law and order is the purpose of two important buildings. The Police Station in Camberwell Church Street has the inscription MP 1898, the date it replaced the first Camberwell Police Station which had been at the corner of Camberwell New Road. The Magistrates' Court at Camberwell Green was erected in 1969.

One important Camberwell building, set on a hillside, with a tower fifty eight metres high, can be seen from far around, the William Booth Memorial College, Champion Park, Denmark Hill. William Booth, founder of the Salvation Army, had dreamed of founding an International University of Humanity. After he died or, as the Salvationists say, was promoted to glory, the College was founded in his memory and opened in 1929. Outside are statues of General Booth and his wife, Catherine, the Army mother. The building was designed by Sir Giles Gilbert Scott, who was architect also of Bankside Power Station. Just as the Salvation Army, under its General, with officers, in uniform, is modelled on a fighting army, so the College was designed to look rather severe, like a barracks. However, the architect, following his grandfather who had designed St Giles Church, favoured the old Gothic style, as can be seen from the stone decoration added over the windows. The Army itself now likes to present a more friendly image. The College trains young men and women from all over the world to become Salvation Army officers.

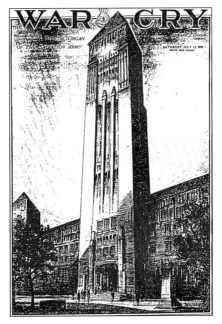

William Booth Memorial College
From War Cry, *magazine of the Salvation Army, July 13th 1929.*

5. ARTS & ENTERTAINMENTS

Gallery and College of Arts

The South London Gallery, Peckham Road, has a history which makes it one of Camberwell's most interesting buildings. Art for the people was its purpose in its early days, over a hundred years ago. It was a pioneer in bringing art and beauty to the poor of South London who had little chance of seeing anything beyond their crowded and dingy back streets. It was supported by many great Victorians, including artists such as Lord Leighton, President of the Royal Academy, and Sir Edward and Lady Burne-Jones, and by the famous actor, Sir Henry Irving. They believed, as Irving said, in a speech to raise funds for the Gallery, "Anyone who sheds a gleam of art on the wintry face of toiling poverty is a benefactor". But the name of William Rossiter, the remarkable man who actually founded the Gallery, deserves to be better known.

Rossiter began in 1868 by setting up a South London Working Men's College. Next came a Free Library, before there were any public libraries in South London. Then, by encouraging artists and others to lend paintings to decorate the walls he soon had a free art gallery. Rossiter's institution was based first in Blackfriars Road and had several moves before finally coming to Camberwell in 1887, temporarily to a warehouse at 207, Camberwell Road. Soon, with the help of a Council, under Lord Leighton, the South London Fine Art Gallery was built in Peckham Road. It opened in 1891. In two ways, especially, the Gallery was in advance of its time. Firstly, it opened on Sundays. Normally the Victorian Sunday was sacred, but it was the only day working people had free. And they came flocking in. Even when the Gallery was still in Camberwell Road, every week about four thousand visitors came on weekdays, and two thousand on Sundays, when music and lectures were also part of the Gallery's attractions. Secondly, the Gallery welcomed children. Years before there were children's libraries they could come to the Gallery to read books, listen to stories, draw, or copy the pictures on the walls. Rossiter described how they were encouraged: "if a poor little ragged monkey, 7 or 8 years old, dressed in a tattered pair of trousers, part of a shirt and one brace, looks in at the door he is asked to come in; he looks curiously and is again invited, and then Miss Olver (the secretary) goes and pulls him in."

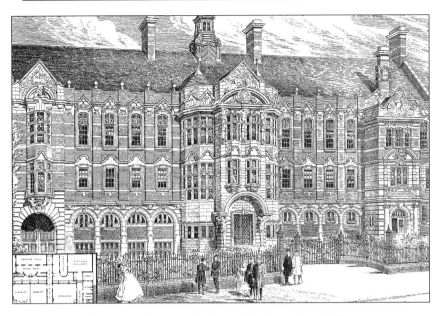

The South London Art Gallery and Camberwell College of Art, 1902
From a drawing by Maurice B Adams, architect.

The inscription over the Gallery entrance reads "The Passmore Edwards South London Art Gallery and Technical Institute". Camberwell has good reason to be grateful to the famous philanthropist, Passmore Edwards, who used the fortune he had made as a newspaper proprietor to help libraries and other institutions. North Camberwell, Dulwich and Nunhead libraries all benefitted from him. In 1893 he provided a rear extension to the South London Gallery for a lecture hall and museum, and then contributed a further sum to build next door what is now Camberwell College of Arts, earlier known as the Passmore Edwards Technical Institute. This became a pioneer in technical education. The grand facade of the Gallery and College, completed in 1898, were designed, like North Camberwell Library, by the architect, Maurice Adams. The Gallery had been transferred to the Camberwell Vestry in 1896 and at first the whole building was under the control of the Vestry and later the Borough Council. Camberwell was the first local authority in London to own an art gallery, museum, and college of art. No wonder the Camberwell coat of arms and the deer and bishop's crook of St Giles are proudly displayed in stone above one entrance. The College, or Technical Institute, however, passed to the London County

Council in 1904 when the LCC became responsible for all public education in London. The extension was built in 1960.

In World War II the Art Gallery was first used as a Food Office, for issuing ration books, but was put out of use in 1941 when bombs destroyed the museum and lecture hall. These have never been rebuilt but the Gallery reopened in 1949. Now, under the London Borough of Southwark, it presents a programme mainly of loan exhibitions, usually the work of present day artists, with an emphasis on those living in Southwark. It still has, however, a large permanent collection of paintings given by its early benefactors, including works by Victorian artists such as John Collier, Val Prinsep and George Watts. Under the present floor boards is an inlaid wood panel by Walter Crane, known to older visitors to the Gallery as The Lily Pond. Later paintings, and also original prints, have been added to the collection. There is an interesting topographical collection of local scenes, many painted before there was photography to record them. They include works by notable artists, including Paul and Thomas Sandby, relatives of George Sandby who was Vicar of St Giles, 1795-1811, and Sir Gerald Kelly, son of a later Vicar.

The Camberwell College of Arts has gained an international reputation. Its prospectus in 1898 said its aim was to "improve the skills of craftsmen". Now it has degree courses in many subjects including ceramics, paper conservation, silversmithing and print making. Camberwell is now part of the London Institute which is made up of several important London art colleges.

Places of entertainment

I'm the Marquis of Camberwell Green
I'm the downiest dude ever seen
I'm a gusher, I'm a rusher
I'm the Marquis of Camberwell Green

Verse from a music hall song

In Victorian Camberwell there was no need to go to London's West End for a good night out. There was plenty of entertainment to be had locally. The earliest music halls were halls attached to pubs, such as The People's

Palace of Varieties, or Lovejoys, at the Rosemary Branch, Southampton Way. In his book, *Peace and dripping toast, memories of the 1890s,* Frederick Willis recalled,

> being taken to one of the last of the old tavern 'free and easies', from which the music hall sprang, at the Rosemary Branch, - - a long, shabby room adjoining the tavern, furnished with chairs and tables and illuminated with flaming gas brackets. At one end - - a stage with footlights screened with blue painted glass. A Chairman sat in front of the stage facing the audience. He wore the most deplorable evening dress. Another gent sat at the piano on the stage. Everybody seemed to be drinking and talking while a man in shirt sleeves was dashing about with a tray loaded with glasses of beer. Each turn was announced by the Chair. He rapped with his hammer both to attract attention and to assist applause. A tall gent sang a song about his wife, his trouble and strife - - .

The Rosemary Branch was finally demolished in 1971. The Castle, on the Castlemead Estate, Camberwell Road, carries on the name of an earlier pub that was the home from 1875 to 1889, of the Bijou Palace of Varieties or Godfrey's Castle Music Hall. One Victorian home of music hall is still standing, the Father Redcap, Camberwell Green. From the outside the pub looks much as when it was rebuilt in 1853. On 2nd December, 1867, the audience here could enjoy "the great W J Collins, a banjoist from America, a Shakespearean sketch, Professor Davis in the renowned rope trick, and Mr Marcus Hellmore in his great delineation of Mephistopholes" The Athenaeum, the learned sounding pub in Camberwell New Road, suggests more high brow activities in that area. Across the road was the Surrey Masonic Hall, home of the South London Institute of Music. Long before television, the Masonic Hall was also used to give people a glimpse of far-away places and events. For example, in 1881, there was on show a "magnificent work of art from the pencils of a number of artists, depicting a voyage around the world, visiting the gorgeous scenery and magnificent cities of China, Japan, India, Persia, Egypt, Australia - with splendid scenes of late events in Afghanistan".

By the 1890s, grand purpose-built theatres were being erected in many London suburbs. Camberwell excelled in having two of these, almost facing each other across Denmark Hill. On the east side was the Oriental Palace of Varieties, built in 1896 by a company under the famous comedian, Dan Leno. In 1899 it was rebuilt as the Camberwell Palace, with seating for over 2,000 people. Famous old timers who appeared here included Marie Lloyd, Harry Lauder, Nellie Wallace and Harry Tate. No wonder Camberwell featured in song. *Chalk Farm to Camberwell Green* by Lionel

Monckton, 1915, is about a young lady who went for a ride on the top of a bus with "a fellow, a regular swell", on what is still the no. 68 bus route. Here is the chorus

> Chalk Farm to Camberwell Green
> All on summer's day
> Up we climbed on the motor bus
> And we started right away
> When we got to the end of the ride
> He asked me to go for a walk!
> But I wasn't Camberwell Green
> By a very long chalk!

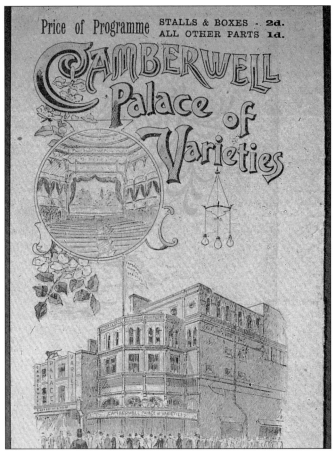

Camberwell Palace of Varieties, c. 1900
From a playbill.

The Camberwell Palace finally closed in 1956. Only a small street named after Orpheus, the musician of ancient Greek legend, marks the site of Camberwell's own music hall. The Metropole, later renamed the Empire, at the corner of Denmark Hill and Coldharbour Lane, was not a music hall, but a high class theatre for plays and opera, opened in 1894 by J B Mulholland, who aimed to bring West End successes to Camberwell. The theatre had a very ornate interior with private boxes, stalls, dress circle, balcony and gallery. Ladies who came in their fashionable hats "were respectfully informed that hats and bonnets are not allowed in the stalls or first two rows of the dress circle".

A little later, in the great days of the cinema, there was plenty of choice, around Camberwell Green for the weekly or twice weekly night out at the pictures. Both the Empire and the Camberwell Palace changed from live entertainment to films. The Empire was rebuilt in 1939 as one of the popular Odeon cinemas, with seating for 2,470. Also on Denmark Hill, on the site of Kwiksave, there was the Golden Domes, later known as the Rex and then as the Essoldo. Across the road, on the site of the Post Office, was the Bijou, known to locals as the Bye Joe. The New Grand Hall Cinematograph Theatre in Camberwell New Road, opened in 1912, had seating for 840 people. The Coronet was a small cinema in Wells Way. With changing times, and the coming of television, all Camberwell's cinemas eventually closed. The Odeon, closed in 1975, was finally demolished in 1994 to build the Foyer. Two cinema buildings are still standing. The Grand, which was closed in 1968, is now a snooker hall. The Regal, Camberwell Road, closed in 1961, is now the Jasmine Bingo Hall.

Finally to something more energetic. One of the first specially built roller-skating rinks in this country opened in 1876 in a large iron building on the east side of Grove Lane, opposite Denmark Hill station. It became known as the Lava Rink when the floor was improved with a layer of lava from Vesuvius. Roller skating was then not just a craze for teenagers. The first English game of roller hockey or rink polo was played here in 1885. Crowds came to watch matches, until the 1914-1918 war, when the rink became a military depot. It was destroyed by fire in about 1920.

6. THE TWENTIETH CENTURY

Camberwell in the wars

Whenever England was at war, Camberwell was prepared to play its part in the defence of the country. In the reign of Queen Elizabeth there were pikemen, billmen and archers ready to face the Spaniards, had the Armada landed, with pikes, bills (hooked sticks) and bows and arrows. Two centuries later, in 1798, the men of Camberwell formed the Camberwell Military Association, one of the volunteer groups raised to meet the threat of invasion by Napoleon. Their commanding officer, at first, was Claude Champion de Crespigny, and later, Colonel Henry Smith of Grove Park. Dr Lettsom was their medical officer. The uniform of the Camberwell Volunteers was a smart blue jacket with scarlet edging, grey trousers and a helmet with a black plume. Their parade ground was at Grove Park. Fortunately, Napoleon was defeated and their military skills were not needed.

The memorial in front of St Giles's Church honours Camberwell's own regiment, the First Surrey Rifles, formed in 1859, which carried on the volunteer tradition. Their motto, Concordia Victrix, inscribed on the memorial, is the same as that embroidered on the colours of the original Camberwell Volunteers. Their headquarters, 1865-1961, were in Flodden Road next to where Volunteers, now known as Territorials, still meet at the Territorial Army Centre. The memorial at St Giles was erected in memory of the men of the First Surrey Rifles, or 21st London Regiment, who gave their lives in World War I, 1914-1918. Added to it are the words, "Also to the memory of our comrades who gave their lives in the World War 1939-1945." Inside the church, in the south transept, is a bronze cabinet transferred from Flodden Road, which contains a book with the names of over a thousand of the regiment who died in the two world wars. The First Surrey Rifles memorial lists their battle honours, in the 1914-18 war, giving some idea of the actions in which the men of Camberwell served, such never to be forgotten names as Loos, Ypres and Mons. The High Wood Barracks in Lordship Lane is named after their courageous attack, in 1916, on a line of enemy forts at High Wood on the River Somme. A second battalion of the regiment served in Greece and the Middle East, Jerusalem and Jericho.

In the first two years of World War I, over 100,000 young men joined up at the Camberwell Town Hall, the chief recruiting station for South London. 4,500 of these were officers and men recruited for Camberwell's own Gun Brigade, the 33rd (Camberwell) Divisional Artillery, raised under the command of Major Fred Hall, MP for Dulwich. Proudly they toured the Camberwell streets, led by their mounted band, before setting off for the Somme, Arras, and Passchendaele. During the war, three Camberwell men won the Victoria Cross. Drummer John Bent got his on 1st November, 1914, when, with all his officers killed, he took command and held his trench at Ypres. Lance Corporal Arthur Cross of the First Surrey Rifles captured two machine guns single-handed on 4th June, 1918. Albert McKenzie, from St Mark's parish, who served in the Royal Navy, in the famous raid on the German submarine and naval base at Zeebrugge on 23rd April, 1918.

"Their name liveth for evermore", is the inscription on the War Memorial in Camberwell Old Cemetery, which lists the names of those from many regiments and the three services who were buried there. Others lie in foreign fields and may have no known graves. What used to be St Mark's Church, Cobourg Road, now overlooks Burgess Park, but was once surrounded by the little back streets of its parish. The sad memorial outside it reads, "In proud and lasting memory of St Mark's Little Army, numbering 4,286. 524 laid down their lives. - - God bless them. May we and England be worthy of them". The memorial outside old St George's Church is a bronze figure of Christ bestowing the Crown of Thorns.

To treat the enormous numbers wounded in World War I, a large part of King's became the Fourth London General Military Hospital. The former St Gabriel's Teachers' Training College in Cormont Road, Lambeth, was turned into another military hospital with huts in Myatts Fields for extra wards. The author, Vera Brittain, was a VAD (Voluntary Aid Detachment) nurse here. In her famous autobiography, *Testament of Youth*, she movingly describes the cold, comfortless nurses' hostel at 31 Champion Hill, the early morning walk down Denmark Hill, because the workmen's trams were full, the arrival at the hospital, often rain-soaked, for 7.00 am breakfast, and then the long day shift, 7.30am to 8.00 pm, nursing young men suffering from horrific wounds.

A Flying Boat in what is now Lucas Gardens, c.1917-18.
Probably the presentation of a Felixstowe F2, or Curtis H series, bought by local
subscription towards the war effort. A backdrop represents the battle front.
In the background are houses in Vestry Road.

Even in World War I, 22 civilians were killed in raids on Camberwell, ten of them when a Zeppelin dropped a bomb, an aerial torpedo, on flats at the corner of Albany Road and Calmington Road.

In World War II, Camberwell was one of the worst hit areas of London. Barrage balloons were a familiar sight, put up to intercept low-flying aircraft. The Platanes, Champion Hill, was the headquarters for the local RAF Balloon Command. Camberwell suffered especially in the Blitz of 1940-41 and then again in 1944-45, the period of the V Is, the flying bombs, or doodle bugs, and the V 2s, the silent rockets. 1,014 residents of the Borough of Camberwell (Camberwell, Peckham and Dulwich) lost their lives in the wartime attacks on London. At least 5,742 were seriously injured. St Giles's Hospital treated many of them. Buildings, such as Chumleigh Gardens in Burgess Park, and Cambridge House, Camberwell Road, were then ARP (Air Raid Precautions) Posts. There were 67 of these throughout Camberwell, in each of which the Warden organised local street patrols, rescue and fire fighting. As the author of *The Battle of South London* wrote at the time, "The exploits of Raleigh and of Drake are chronicled for all time but beside them might well be chronicled the exploits of the men and women who inhabit our small streets."

Many children were evacuated to escape the bombing. On September 1st, 1939, children from St George's School caught the train at Denmark Hill Station for Sevenoaks - not to prove a very safe area a year later, after the fall of France. So, in June 1940, there was a second evacuation, this time to Bideford in Devon, where the children were billeted on village families and learnt something of country life. Their teacher, Fred Nichols, returning one day to his Camberwell school, found his classroom wrecked by bomb blast. Some children were not evacuated, preferring to stay at home with their parents. Alf Slater, who lived at Evelina Mansions, New Church Road, was twelve when war began. His block of flats had a shelter in the basement area, just below street level, 20 feet long and 6 feet high, with three long wooden forms to sit on. As he wrote later, "Lack of sleep became a way of life". One night he "thought the shelter was to be my tomb".

> We could hear the menacing growl of the bombers approaching and the bangs of our own guns. - - The heavy throbbing of the engines came very loud and directly overhead - Everything happened so quickly - the explosion stung our ears - The next one produced much the same effect, but the light appeared to dance a crazier pattern. We then had - a huge rush of wind. A peculiar type of pressure seemed to invade the shelter. - - I was transformed with terror as the frightening aftermath began. There was a chaos of noise as shattered windows spewed broken glass and bricks and rubbish came thudding down on the roof of the shelter. - - My mother caught my arm and held me - We braced ourselves for the impending avalanche, sure the flats would descend on us and that we would be buried under their crushing mass. Would the shelter hold the weight? -Perhaps we would be choked with dust and unable to call out to the rescue men to tell them where we were. These were some of the terrified thoughts that invaded my mind.

Fortunately that bomb had fallen in the middle of the road, though the edge of the crater was only twelve feet from the shelter. Alf lived to tell the tale in the book, *The times of our lives.*

Shelters were indeed no protection against a direct hit. On 17th September, 1940, nine members of one family from Medlar Street, Sidney and Elizabeth Wright, their five young daughters, and their son and his wife, both aged only 21, were all killed in a public shelter on Camberwell Green. They were buried in Camberwell New Cemetery where their names are recorded on the memorial set up in 1995 to those who have no marked grave. Others died in the streets. On 29th December, 1940, for example, most of the casualties were the passengers and crew of trams, stopped outside the Town Hall, when bombs dropped on Peckham Road. During the second period of bombing, the V 1s and V 2s were especially damaging to property.

Over 2,000 men, employed by the Council, worked constantly on repairs. DIY materials were also issued along with tarpaulins to keep out the rain. Nearly all the houses in Camberwell were damaged in some way during the war, and 5,650 were totally destroyed.

In World War II the First Surrey Rifles became an anti-aircraft battalion to defend the country from enemy bombers. As in earlier wars, Camberwell men and women did their bit in all the services towards ensuring victory. One of the heroes was Corporal Sydney Bates, son of a Camberwell rag and bone man who, at Caen in Normandy, not long after D-Day, bravely led an attack on the enemy and, though three times wounded, fought on until they withdrew. The action cost him his life but gained him the Victoria Cross. The inscription on his grave in the War Cemetery at Bayeux, reads "His parents proudly remember him as a true Camberwell boy and a loving son".

New Housing - New Space

If someone who left Camberwell before World War II were to come back now, he or she would find parts of it almost unrecognisable. Many people are living in housing which is not only new, but of a totally different type, with tall blocks unimagined in the past. Small streets, especially in North Camberwell, have disappeared, giving way to huge housing estates or to create a vast new open space, Burgess Park.

At the end of the war large numbers of people were in urgent need of housing. Many houses had been destroyed and no new ones had been built. In addition, people living in slums needed better conditions. An enormous building programme was begun and Council housing, mainly blocks of flats, took over much of Camberwell. Even before the war, the LCC had replaced old houses on Peckham Road with the Glebe Estate. After 1945, Camberwell Borough Council began by infilling bomb sites, for example, in Camberwell Grove, where four-storey 1950s flats break the line of Georgian houses. The problem was how to deal with the thousands still on the housing waiting list. Architects, making use of the new materials now available, pre-cast concrete slabs instead of bricks, thought they had the answer. It was tower blocks. These, so it was believed, would make as much use as possible of the land available, allow for public open space around them, and give the residents plenty of light, air and distant views, unlike their crowded back streets. Sceaux Gardens, built mainly in the grounds of the old Camberwell House, Peckham Road, was the first estate in Camberwell, and one of the first in London, to have tower blocks, two of fourteen storeys each, as well as other blocks of more ordinary height. Other tower-blocks soon followed, such as the eighteen storey Castlemead, on the west side of Camberwell Road. Meanwhile, the LCC and, after 1965, the GLC was busy with slum clearance. The Wyndham and Comber estates replaced the poor housing between Camberwell Road and Camberwell New Road, with what Pevsner calls "lumpy tower blocks, in the brutalist style of the LCC Architects' Department at that time". The Elmington Estate, between Camberwell Road and Southampton Way, was another large area cleared and redeveloped by the LCC with tower blocks. It has about 700 dwellings.

Sceaux Gardens Estate, 1959.

Tower blocks however soon went out of fashion. People who had to live in them realised they were far from ideal homes, especially for families with children. The Gloucester Grove Estate, St George's Way, is only

6 storeys though, originally not very welcoming in appearance. Pevsner described it as "a fortress-like chain of six storey slabs linked by yellow brick staircase drums". It also had the faults of many estates of the 1970s. Its GLC architects, concerned to separate pedestrians from the ever increasing traffic of the roads, linked the separate blocks with long walkways, high above ground level. No-one realised at first that residents might be in even more danger from muggers and vandals on foot than from the motor car. However, recently, things have improved on part of the estate. Gloucester Grove is one of five estates in Camberwell and Peckham chosen for a special Regeneration Programme, funded by the Department of the Environment, Southwark Council, housing associations, and business firms. Gone are the long internal walkways. The line of buildings is now broken by gleaming glass cylinders instead of yellow brick drums. They enclose entrance halls with lifts to the various floors. Entry phones and videos control access. The estate is now surrounded by gardens and play areas. The estate will eventually house only about half the number of people crowded into it originally. Gloucester Grove has recently received a Royal Institute of British Architects award for its improvements. Since 1980, like all Council housing, it has come under Southwark Council.

The Selborne Estate is a private development tucked away near Camberwell Green. It seems like a village with its footpaths, small brick houses and pretty front gardens. It was opened in 1982 and marked a turning point in the modern development of Camberwell. Before this, whole streets of older houses had been cleared. In spite of protests, this is what had happened to Selbourne Road and other Victorian streets nearby. But times had changed, and money was lacking to build a big council estate. The site was sold and on it were built the kind of homes most people like. From then on, developments were small scale, mostly houses, rather than flats, and for owner occupiers or housing associations, rather than council tenants. Older houses too, that had survived the war and the developers, were now admired and, where possible, refurbished. Jephson Street, off Grove Lane, is a good example. It was restored by a housing association for students at the Camberwell College of Arts. With its Victorian-style lamp posts, it looks much as it was when really new. Hopewell Yard, interestingly designed housing off Elmington Road, uses the ground plan and some old buildings of what was once the stable yard of Carter Paterson's, the famous removals firm. Albany Mews, Albany Road, was once a stable block for the big houses of Camberwell Road.

Just to show the wheel has turned full circle; plans for the Gloucester Grove Estate include demolishing some blocks which have not been modernised and replacing them with terraced housing. Some older Camberwell residents may well remember similar houses that were demolished to build the estate only about thirty years ago!

Names chosen for new housing usually have some meaning. Gloucester Grove Estate took its name from one of the streets south of St George's Way that was demolished. The street itself was named after the long ago Lord of the Manor, the Earl of Gloucester. The names chosen for the estate are those of Gloucestershire villages. The small part of the old street left standing, has been renamed after one of them, Newent Close. Its charming early 19th century villas, with the huge estate in the background, sum up, at a glance, the history of this part of Camberwell. The Glebe Estate, on ancient glebe land, has the names of early vicars of St Giles, such as Philip de Longleigh, vicar 1322-1338 and John Bodeney, 1393-8. The Comber Estate, remembering Thomas Comber, has the names of missionaries and explorers, for example, Livingstone, Moffat and Speke. Poets and writers, such as Keats, Kipling, Milton and Herrick, feature on the Elmington Estate, not far from where Robert Browning, was born. Crawford Estate, off Coldharbour Lane, has the names of fairs, for example, Bartholomew and Widdecombe, in memory of the Camberwell Fair. Names on the Sceaux Gardens Estate are associated with the history of Sceaux, a suburb of Paris, with which the Borough of Camberwell had a Friendship Link. Marie Curie, discoverer of radium, lived in Sceaux. Colbert, chief minister of King Louis XIV, rebuilt its chateau.

"The most incredible park in London". That is how Burgess Park is described in the book, *A walk round London parks*. Its author, Hunter Davies, says this because the park was not, like many others, such as Peckham Rye, old farm or common land that had never been built on. In Burgess Park "the whole process was turned upside down". A whole built-up area, 30 streets, 900 dwellings, schools, churches, factories, etc. was bulldozed to produce this open space. Plans for such a park go back to the 1943 *County of London Plan.* Its authors, J H Forshaw and P Abercrombie, saw that the whole area from the Thames, south to Camberwell Green, was one mass of streets with almost no open space. Their bold plan was to provide a green lung, stretching from Camberwell Road to Old Kent Road, on the line of the Grand Surrey Canal, bounded by Albany Road on the north and St George's Road on the south, 135 acres (51 hectares) in all. It would serve not only Camberwell, but also Southwark, Lambeth and Lewisham. Gloucester Grove and the Peckham estates, to the south, and Aylesbury to the north, were designed with little open space of their own because they were so near to the park - small comfort for the first residents since it was reckoned that completion of the park would take 50 years!

Land was acquired gradually. Off Addington Square there was already a very small park, King George's Field, opened in 1937, as a memorial to King George V. Its gateposts can still be found, inscribed with the lion and unicorn of the royal coat of arms. Then came sites where buildings did not need much demolition. Hitler's bombs had done that job or, at least, left them damaged and derelict. For years the North Camberwell Open Space, as it was called, was just a jigsaw of small plots of grass between old streets and buildings, together with the site of the canal, closed in 1970. By 1982, often by compulsory purchase, the pieces of the jigsaw had been joined together and the park was complete. Sadly, in the process, some people who had lived all their lives in well cared for houses, and well loved streets, saw their old homes destroyed. In 1974, the Open Space was named Burgess Park, after Alderman Mrs Jessie Burgess, CBE, a lady who had given great service to the local community. She was Camberwell's first woman Mayor, 1945-47 and a Council member for 44 years. Her husband was Mayor 1947-49.

When the London Borough of Southwark inherited the park from the GLC in 1986, it already had a children's play centre in Albany Road, a huge lake, for fishing and boating, near the Old Kent Road, tennis courts and football pitches. Trees have been planted, at least fifteen different species from many parts of the world, such as a dawn redwood, a tree of heaven, and a Himalayan birch, and a whole avenue of willows of the type used to make cricket bats. Further progress in developing the park to its full potential has however sometimes seemed slow, though now, things are looking up. At Chumleigh Gardens there is a visitor centre and exhibitions. Educational activities encourage inner city children to study wild life. In 1995 the management of the park was handed over to the Southwark Groundwork Trust, one of thirty such trusts across the country set up to improve the local environment. It has funding from the Department of the Environment, Southwark Council and business firms. Perhaps, by the Millennium, Burgess Park, after over fifty years, will be a dream come true.

Pioneering Institutions

In 1991, according to the census, 1677 people living in the St Giles and Brunswick wards of Camberwell were unemployed, about 15% of the total population. Drinkers and social misfits are apt to gather on Camberwell Green. Crime is a problem in the area, although a campaign is at present underway to combat it. As in the 19th century, so in the late 20th, Camberwell has plenty of the problems and human tragedies of the inner-city. It also has a number of institutions which have been pioneers in meeting these problems and improving the general quality of life. One, Cambridge House, set up to help the poor of Victorian Camberwell is still, after over 100 years, doing good work today, adapting itself to new circumstances and needs. It began in 1889 as one of the first of the university settlements, an important movement at that time when it was only the wealthy who could go to university. A settlement consisted of a group of young men from Oxford or Cambridge who felt it was their Christian duty to bridge the gap between themselves and those less fortunate by going to live in a poor part of London, providing leadership and help to local people. There were several settlements in Southwark, for example Pembroke College Mission, Walworth. Trinity College, Cambridge, took over the care of St George's parish, Camberwell . The two Georgian houses in Camberwell Road, which it leased as accommodation for volunteers from the college, soon became known as Cambridge House. Talbot House, Addington Square was similar, but a women's settlement. The two settlements amalgamated in 1972.

From the beginning there have been activities at Cambridge House, or organised by its members, for all ages, but especially for young people. In the early years there were boys' clubs, girls' clubs, cricket, football and summer camps. In 1893 Cambridge House helped to start Hollington Boys Club, Comber Grove, which is still going strong. Cambridge House was, and still is, the local centre for the Children's Country Holiday Fund. By 1908 the Fund was sending away annually almost 2,000 children. According to an early Magazine, "the development of such children during a fortnight's country holiday is one of the most pathetic and wonderful things to be seen in the House's work". In 1948 Cambridge House opened the first adventure playground in this country, on a bomb site in Camberwell. There are today more than sixty such playgrounds in the London area. At Cambridge House there is now a pre-school playgroup, a Saturday Arts

Club for 5-12 year olds, a rhythmic gymnastic club for ages 5-25 and holidays for young people at its own country campsite. A Neighbourhood Development Project works with Tenants' Associations to provide evening and summer activities on local estates.

The "Poor Man's Lawyer", free professional legal advice, was one of the earliest services available at Cambridge House. In 1994 the Cambridge House Legal Centre helped 1,534 people who could not afford legal fees, but had urgent problems, for example, facing possible eviction from their homes. There is also an independent advocacy scheme to advise people needing community care. Adult education was another early concern of Cambridge House. It ran evening classes for those who then had no chance of further education after leaving elementary school. Now, higher education is provided elsewhere, but in 1963 Cambridge House realised some adults had a more basic need. They could not read or write. It set up one of the first literacy schemes, a model soon to be followed by others. The Adult Education Project now teaches literacy, numeracy, use of computers and also English for speakers of other languages. For people with learning

Cambridge House, 1891.

difficulties Cambridge House has various projects. Only Connect, a children's holiday scheme, People to People, for those over nineteen, and the Camberwell Advocacy Office to speak for those who cannot always speak up for themselves. Cambridge House is also a meeting place for the Friday Community Club and for many outside organisations.

Over the years, though its work has gone on, the character of Cambridge House has changed. The last of the residents moved out in the 1980's. It now describes itself as a "locally managed, multi-purpose, social action and community education centre". It relies on paid professional staff helped by an army of volunteers who come, not from a distant Cambridge College but from the neighbourhood it serves. It is a registered charity but has some funding from Southwark Council. Like other voluntary organisations, it now provides some of those services which might at one time have been provided directly by the local authority.

St Giles's Trust, another pioneering institution, began in 1961 as the Camberwell Samaritans, meeting at St Giles's Vicarage. In 1964 the church cleared its crypt of coffins and opened it as a day centre for the single homeless, one of the first in London. Over thirty years later, in 1995, sadly more needed than ever, the centre, after much fund-raising, moved to pleasant new premises in Camberwell Church Street. It now welcomes not only those actually homeless but all vulnerable people. Here, in addition to such basics as food, showers, laundry and a few hours of safe warm haven from the streets, attenders receive housing advice and healthcare. There are sessions for those with alcohol or drug problems and the Centre provides, for some, the Care in the Community needed after the closure of the big mental hospitals. There are also literacy, art and life skills classes and other activities. About 100 people a day attend the Centre, as many as the staff and building can cope with. The Centre has support from Southwark Council, health authorities, government departments and charities. The Camberwell Credit Union, a self-help savings and loans scheme, also began at St Giles's Church. It was founded in the crypt in 1974, the first credit union in Southwark and one of the first in the country.

The Camberwell Circle Trust, based in Camberwell Grove, was founded in 1964, originally as a centre, somewhat similar to that at St Giles, but since 1979 it has been providing what most of its members needed most, which was housing. It now has sixteen houses in Camberwell, Peckham and Brixton for single homeless men and women, age 21-55. All Circle residents have other needs besides housing, for example problems with drink or drugs, HIV, mental health problems, or disabilities. They may be the victims of violence or abuse or ex-prisoners trying to restart their lives. Housing Managers give them support and advice on how to live as independently as possible, so that they may be ready to move on from this short-term housing to more permanent accommodation which they are helped to obtain from the Council or housing associations.

As a building, the Foyer, at the junction of Denmark Hill and Coldharbour Lane, opened in 1995, is the most striking recent addition to the Camberwell scene. Its purpose is even more important and imaginative. Since 1969 the charity Centrepoint has been providing overnight shelter for young people sleeping rough in the London streets. The Foyer, managed by Centrepoint, provides for their longer term needs. Based on a French concept it is the first of its type in this country. Its aim is to break the tragic cycle of, no home, no job, no job, no home. The building is both a hostel where the 80 young residents each have a bed-sit in two-person flats, and also provides for them a training and job-search centre. The Junction, a public restaurant, is all part of the Foyer concept.

Love Walk is the oldest foundation in Camberwell for those with physical disabilities. In its time this too was a pioneer, founded in 1912, before many people were aware of the real needs of disabled people. Its founder, Alice Blanche, had seen young disabled girls obliged to spend all their lives in hospitals because they had nowhere to go and no means of earning a living. Her Home for Invalid Women Workers provided the residents with a place to live, a training in fine needlecraft, and a workshop which became famous for the beautiful items it produced. However, times change. Since 1975, Love Walk has taken men as well as women residents. With many careers now open to people with disabilities, the workshop closed, replaced by an activity room with classes in various subjects. Residents are encouraged to be as independent as possible. In place of the dormitories of the early days they each have their own flat or bed-sit from which they can make their way by wheelchair to the nearby shops. Good Neighbours House, Mary Datchelor Close, opened in 1979 as the first purpose-built home in Europe for people suffering from cerebral palsy. Supported originally by stars of the stage, it is now run by the charity Scope.

Multi-cultural Camberwell

The Multi-cultural Gardens at Chumleigh Gardens, in Burgess Park, aim to represent the plants and gardens found in the countries of origin of people who now live in Southwark. There is an Oriental Garden, with rocks and water and, of course, the tea plant. Grapes and olives grow in the Mediterranean Garden. The African and Caribbean Garden has tropical plants, bamboos, arum lilies, and the cactus of the desert regions. The Islamic Garden, with its pond, palm trees, and blue patterned tiles, has a cool atmosphere, welcome even here in the hot summer of 1995 when the gardens were opened. The central courtyard of Chumleigh Gardens is laid out as an English garden. Like most English gardens, it not only has truly native plants, but others which now seem native, but really were brought into this country at some time in the past.

These gardens reflect well multi-cultural Southwark and especially multi-cultural Camberwell. People from overseas have been coming to Camberwell for a very long time. Some of the first to come were the Huguenots from France, the de Crespignys and the Minets, who became great landowners in Camberwell and Lambeth. Barraud is another Huguenot name. It is well known in the history of clockmakers, stained-glass manufacturers and artists. The family is mainly associated with Lambeth but some of them lived on Champion Hill. Small roundels with angels survive of the stained glass in St Giles's Church by the firm of Lavers and Barraud. The memorial window to William Barraud, painter of horses and dogs, was destroyed in the war. Henry Gastineau, another artist of Huguenot descent, lived in Coldharbour Lane, 1827-76. One of his local scenes is in the South London Gallery.

The first reference to Germans in Camberwell is in a curious little pamphlet, *The State of the Palatines for fifty years past to this present time,* published in 1710, and one of the oldest items in the Local Studies Library. It has a picture of German Protestant refugees living in tents in Camberwell and Blackheath. About 9,000 had been forced to flee their homes in the district known as the Palatinate, Rhineland and Bavaria, by the French King, Louis XIV. They were kindly treated in Camberwell, where Mr Cock was a trustee of the relief fund and the church wardens hired barns to house them. Many eventually left for new lives in Ireland, America and the West Indies. In Victorian times there was a large colony of Germans living in Camberwell, some of them very wealthy. These lived mainly in the Denmark Hill area. The name "Osnabruck", after a German town, is still just readable on the gatepost of what was 105 Denmark Hill. In 1888 this was the home of a Fritz Rommel. There was a German church in Windsor Walk, site now of an extension to the Maudsley Hospital. In 1875, according to Blanch, there were about eighty families belonging to it, "principally persons of substantial means". In 1842 the great musician, Mendelssohn, visited one of the local German families, the Beneckes, relations of his wife, at their home on Denmark Hill. It was here that he composed one of his *Songs without words,* now known as the *Spring Song.* Its original title was *Camberwell Green.* Wagner was another of the Beneckes' musical visitors. Their house was one of eight demolished to make Ruskin Park. Its site, near the south end of the Park, is marked by a small pedestal (sadly, once a sundial).

Many of the residents of Champion Hill at one time were Germans, or naturalised Germans, with business interests in London. Most of the grand houses where they once lived have now gone. One still standing is The Platanes. The name is in fact German (and Latin) for the plane trees which still shade its front garden. The house, built in 1882, was bought, in 1890, by Herman Kleinworth, a great merchant banker, a founder of the firm which is now Kleinwort Benson. At The Platanes, he and his family lived in style. The house had a ballroom and a winter garden and in its grounds were stables for the horses and the carriage which took Kleinworth to the City. There were cottages for the coachman and for the gardener who looked after the greenhouse and orchard. Herman Kleinworth's neighbours were mostly relations. Next door was the home of his sister, Mrs Andreae, on the site of Ruskin Court. Another sister, Mrs Wilhelmina Martin, lived across the road at Redcourt, now also replaced with modern housing. The Denner family, cousins of Mrs Kleinworth, lived at a house on the site of 35 Champion Hill and next door to them was her uncle, Carl Gunther, from Antwerp. After he moved away in 1908, Kleinworth gave The Platanes to King's College, and since then it has been a students' hostel.

Not all the German residents of Camberwell were wealthy. Many were simply small tradesmen. When war broke out in 1914, Germany became the hated enemy and everywhere there were attacks on these enemy aliens, even though they had lived peacefully in this country most of their lives. Their names were enough to give them away, if they had not changed them. George Melsheimer of Albany Road, and Emil Eifler of Camberwell

Green, both butchers, and J Sturmer and Mr Frieburger of Camberwell Road, and Mr Moth of Wyndham Road, bakers, were all attacked and had their windows smashed and shops wrecked. Eventually, all German men who had not been naturalised were deported, thus ending the German community in Camberwell. Even street names were changed. Leipsic Road, named after the German town, became Comber Grove.

Irish people came to London in the 19th century to find work, mainly building the docks, the canal, and the railways. Many lived in the poorest part of Camberwell, the Sultan Street area. Irish are still coming here. In the 1991 Census, 1066 people out of the 20,975 living in the two wards which cover most of Camberwell, St Giles and Brunswick, registered as born in Ireland.

Many people from Cyprus live in Camberwell. They come from an island that was once under British rule and is still a member of the Commonwealth. Some were sadly uprooted in 1974 when Cyprus was partitioned between Greeks and Turks. There is a Bank of Cyprus on Denmark Hill. Christian Greek Cypriots worship at the Greek Orthodox Cathedral in Camberwell New Road. Their children keep up their mother tongue with Greek classes held there on Saturdays. Turkish Cypriots are mostly Moslem. What was once St Mark's Church, Coburg Road, is now the New Peckham Mosque and a meeting place for the London Islamic Turkish Association.

People of African, Caribbean or Asian origin are naturally the most noticeable of those who, over the years, have made their homes in Camberwell. Most have come since World War II but one Jamaican, Dr Harold Moody, important enough to have an entry in the *Dictionary of National Biography*, came to England in 1904. After qualifying at King's College Hospital, he set up in practice in Peckham, where he was a well-loved doctor. He is famous as a pioneer in the campaign to improve the status of black people and abolish racial distinction and lectured on the subject here and in the USA and the West Indies. In 1931 he founded the League of Coloured Peoples at his home, 164 Queen's Road, Peckham, now marked with a blue plaque. For twenty five years, until his death in 1947, he was a member of the Camberwell Green Congregational Church. The minister of the church wrote his biography, *Negro victory.*

The first big influx of West Indians came by ship, the Empire Windrush, which docked at Tilbury in 1948. For one of them, Sam King, this was a

Sam King, Mayor of Southwark, 1983-4.

return journey. He had been a leading aircraftsman stationed in Britain during the war and came to rejoin the RAF. Later he worked for the Post Office. By 1950 he had bought a house in Sears Street, New Church Road, and set up a scheme to help other black immigrants to get their own homes. He was one of those who started the first West Indian Carnival and the first black newspaper, the *West Indian Gazette*. He was elected to Southwark Council in 1982 and, in 1983, became Southwark's first black mayor, and at that time, the only black mayor in Britain. His ideals are those of a Christian Socialist and he left Southwark to become a Pentecostal minister. In the 1991 Census, 2,267 Camberwell residents, just over 10% of the total population, described themselves as black Caribbean. Black Africans, and other black people, make up another 2,390, about 11%. Black Christians now form part of the congregations of most Camberwell churches, for example, St Giles. Others belong to black-led churches, mainly Pentecostal, which have often taken over older church buildings. The Calvary Temple, New Church Road, is now a meeting place for the United Pentecostals and the former Presbyterian Church in Benhill Road is now the Elim Pentecostal. The Bethel United Church of Jesus Christ Apostolic meets in St Giles's Church Hall.

Many Indians living in Uganda came to this country in the 1970s, expelled by the dictator, Idi Amin. Some of these are among the 757 Indians, Pakistanis, Bangladeshis, and other Asians living in Camberwell. There are also 372 Chinese. There is a Southwark Hindu Centre in Benhill Road. A number of organisations in Camberwell provide meeting points or advice centres for various ethnic groups, such as the Southwark Asian Women's Group, the Southwark African Organisation, the Southwark Black Education Group, the national Afro-Asian Advisory Centre for immigration and nationality problems, the British Somali Southwark Refugee Council, and the Mauritius Association. There are two multi-racial theatre and arts projects, the Umoja Theatre Company, Bethwin Road and the Black Heroes Project, Benhill Road.

The place really to get the feel - and the taste - of multi-cultural Camberwell today is around Camberwell Green. Nobody who shops there can fail to notice the variety of peoples among their fellow shoppers. Nearly all the small shops, helpfully kept open at unsocial hours, are either continental grocers and greengrocers run mostly by Cypriots, or news agents and sweet shops kept by Asians. Apart from these, every other business seems to be a restaurant, serving some country's distinctive cuisine. Greek Cyprus is represented by the Lemon Grove and the Vineyard, and Turkish by the Bolu Kebab and the Fez. The Indian sub-continent and Ugandan Asians are represented by Zara's Kitchen, Joy Bangla Curry House, and several Tandooris, such as the Noor Balti and the Nogar. The West Indian taste is catered for with the Cousin Creole and a Jamaican take-away. There is also the Spanish Marbella Hotel with its tapas bar, the Brazilian Minuano and, in Southampton Way, the Sopar Thai Restaurant and the Cafe Mexicano. As everywhere, there are plenty of Chinese take-aways and restaurants with such exotic names as Silver Lake and Peach Blossom. There are naturally lots of places to buy pizzas, burgers, and kebabs, fast-foods all introduced from abroad in recent years, but now seemingly as English as the fish and chips sold by Andrews, one of the few such shops to survive. In fact, why go abroad? Abroad has come to Camberwell!

7. POSTSCRIPT

Camberwell: an historic community

Camberwell, as an historic community, must be one of the best served by historians of all the old villages that now make up the greater London area. Recorded by the 17th century John Aubrey and the great 18th century antiquaries, Lysons and Manning and Bray, by 1841 it already had its first real local historian, Douglas Allport. His book, *Collections illustrative of the geology, history, antiquities and associations of Camberwell and its neighbourhood*, is based firstly on a great deal of research. It quotes early books, local records and obscure documents at the Public Record Office. Of equal importance, however, is Allport's own accurate knowledge of his native parish at a crucial time in its development from village to suburb; a time when, as he writes, "the unusual spectacle has been presented of two fields of very fine wheat immediately adjoining the high road, and completely surrounded by houses." Illustrations are from his own drawings, mostly of buildings now long gone, such as Bowyer House, Champion Lodge, and old St. Giles. He was an eye-witness to the fire which destroyed it.

Allport was born in Peckham. A plaque on the south wall of St. Giles's churchyard commemorates his father-

> Near this place lies the body of Thomas Allport of Peckham in the parish, sometime merchant of the City of London, who was born in Staffordshire in 1758 and died at Peckham, 2nd November 1818. Also that of Martha, his wife, - - who died at Camberwell, 24th March 1833.

Douglas, born 1803, was the fourteenth of their seventeen children. He attended Thomas Ready's school, Peckham, and later Dr Wanostrocht's Academy and then, like his father, worked in the City. The family were members of the Mansion House Chapel. Douglas helped with the Nelson Street School and was a founder of the Camberwell Literary Institute which met at Bowyer House. Denison Howard Allport, his great-great nephew, was author of *Wilson's Grammar School* and of several books on Dulwich. From 1806 to 1948, when he moved away, the Allport family played a notable part in Camberwell life.

William Harnett Blanch
From South London Press*, June 16th, 1900.*

The name Blanch must be familiar to anyone interested in Camberwell history. His monumental tome *Ye Parish of Camberwell* published in 1875, is a mine of information on Camberwell, Peckham and Dulwich. As a local government officer, an Assistant Overseer of the Camberwell Vestry, William Harnett Blanch had access to all kinds of local archives such as *Vestry Minutes* and *Churchwardens' Accounts*. He also spent two summer vacations at St Giles's Church studying the *Parish Registers* which were then stored in the vestry. The long extracts transcribed from such records make not only interesting reading, but are a very convenient source of material for the local historian. Blanch also gives up-to-date, that is 1875, information on the churches, schools, institutions and charities of his own time. No wonder that, in appreciation of his work for Camberwell, "a perfect galaxy of literary, scientific, artistic and local celebrities" entertained him to a testimonial dinner at the Crystal Palace on 28th July 1877. His friend, W F Noble, who helped him with research at the British Museum and the Public Record Office and compiled the index to the book, produced a 16 volume version of it, interleaved with insertions down to 1912. This is now at the Minet Library, Lambeth. Blanch and his wife, who "undertook correspondence and made hundreds of calls to collect information", lived at 55 Denman Road, Peckham. They had six children. He was a fellow of the Royal Historical Association. His other writings include, *Dulwich College and Edward Alleyn*, and *School Life in Christ's Hospital*, of which he was an old boy. He also produced booklets on rating assessment, and articles in the *South London Press*. He died in 1900, aged 64.

H J Dyos, Professor of Urban History at Leicester University, very fortunately chose Camberwell as the field for his research. His book *Victorian Suburb; a study of the growth of Camberwell*, which came out in 1961, broke new ground with its detailed analysis of how a suburb develops, a subject which had been largely ignored by historians before his time. After reading it one looks at Camberwell and then at any suburb of London or other great city with new understanding. Using an enormous amount of original material such as house auction details, vestry reports and parliamentary papers, the book makes it possible to find out how, when and why a particular area or street was built up at a particular time. *Exploring the Urban Past*, edited by David Cannadine and David Reeder is a collection of other writings by H J Dyos. Sadly he died in 1978, aged 57, before he could write a second book on Camberwell.

Today it is mainly members of the Camberwell Society who continue the work of the great historians. Nearly every quarterly newsletter contains an article of original scholarly research into some aspect of Camberwell history. The first editor, Stephen Marks, used his architectural expertise in the study of Camberwell's Georgian period and also brought to light a wealth of material relating to Camberwell, including the earliest known map of any part of it, *Friern Manor, 1739*, which he discovered at the British Museum. Articles by the present editor, Tony Wilson, on such subjects as the Greek Orthodox church, Denmark Hill Grammar School, St Giles's Hospital and Germans in Camberwell have provided the material for many of the later chapters in *The Story of Camberwell*.

Camberwell's past has certainly been well researched and recorded. It also has a rich architectural heritage from that past with no fewer than five Conservation Areas: Addington Square, Camberwell Green, Camberwell Grove, Camberwell New Road and Sceaux Gardens, which includes the 18th century buildings north and south of Peckham Road and the Gallery and College of Art. There are two other Conservation Areas which overlap its borders, Coburg Road and Grosvenor Park.

Camberwell, however, is not just a place with a history. It is a live community today. Its central feature is still Camberwell Green, a legacy from its earliest years. The main roads which intersect there may now be rather shabby due to years of blight caused by successive road and traffic schemes which came to nothing. Nevertheless they have many assets for local people, a variety of restaurants, a modern shopping centre, Butterfly Walk opened in 1985, and a number of long-established specialist shops. Duraty's Radio and Television shop on Denmark Hill was founded in 1925, in the early days of the wireless, as the Durable Accumulator Company Ltd, and is still a family firm. Kembers and Lawrence, the chemists, have been at Camberwell Green for about seventy years. Howards the builders' merchants and ironmongers have been in Coldharbour Lane since 1950. Pesh Flowers have been brightening the scene on Denmark Hill for over thirty years. Kennedy's have been supplying their well known sausages and pies at their Denmark Hill shop since the 1920s and Great Expectations, the picture framers, opened in 1960. There is a good second-hand bookshop, the Camberwell Bookshop in Camberwell Grove. Camberwell Green itself had a face lift in 1995 with new lighting and hanging flower baskets and soon it is hoped there will be further improvements.

Many organisations help to give Camberwell a sense of community, the newly formed Camberwell Traders Association, the Camberwell Policing Community Group, Camberwell Tennis Club, Camberwell Gardens Guild, Camberwell Pocket Opera and the Camberwell Choir School for young singers, based at St Giles's Church. The Camberwell Society, an exceptionally active and able amenity society has been safeguarding the development and heritage of Camberwell since 1970. One of its earliest victories was the preservation of Addington Square, threatened with demolition for inclusion in Burgess Park. It also encourages the arts and local businesses, supports charities and has a stimulating programme of meetings for local people.

With its history, heritage and community life, Camberwellians have many reasons to be proud of their own London village. To treat it at all adequately in a small book is even more impossible now than it was 120 years ago when Blanch set out to write "a shilling history" and ended up with a volume of over 600 pages!

Sources and suggestions for further reading

Some sources used for this book are given below. They are available for reference at Southwark Local Studies Library, 211 Borough High Street, London SE1 1JA (Tel: 0171 403 3507). This has a comprehensive collection of books, maps, illustrations, press cuttings, archives and microfilms (of census returns, local newspapers, etc.) Opening hours obtainable from any library. An appointment is not necessary except for consultation of archives, use of microfilm reader, or for school party visits. Some items are in print or available through lending libraries.

GENERAL

Douglas Allport - *Camberwell, 1841.*

W H Blanch - *Camberwell,* 1875, reprinted Camberwell Society, 1976.

Camberwell Quarterly; newsletter of Camberwell Society, 1970 to date.

B Cherry & N Pevsner - *The buildings of England; London South,* Penguin, 1983.

H J Dyos - *Victorian Suburb; a study of the growth of Camberwell,* Leicester UP, 1961.

1. EARLY DAYS

R J Warhurst - *A view of Dulwich, Peckham and Camberwell in 1300,* 2nd ed, 1992.

John Rocque - *Map of London and 10 miles around, 1741-5.* 1746

A survey of the whole Manor of Frerne 1739, copied 1799. British Museum Maps.

36 Grove Lane, 1720-1792; 177-183 Camberwell Grove, 1720-1931; deeds.

D H Allport - *Wilson's Grammar School, including Greencoat School,* 1984.

G F Prosser - *St Giles Church, Camberwell, 1827.*

James Jonathan Abraham - *Lettsom,* Heinemann, 1933. chap. xvi.

Philippa Glanville - *The plate purchases of a Tudor lawyer* (John Bowyer) LMAS 1978.

J Edwards - *A Companion from London to Brighthelmstone, 1801, appendix 1819.*

Sir Thomas Smyth, Camberwell Survey, 1830; Minet Estate plans 1769-1839; Estates of Sir Claude Champion de Crespigny, 1840. Lambeth Archives.

Handbills for *Camberwell Fair, Royal Flora Gardens,* and *Rosemary Branch.*

2. INTO THE MODERN ERA

Dept of the Environment - *List of buildings of special architectural or historic interest.*

J Dewhirst - *Map of the Parish of St Giles, 1842.* Reprinted by Camberwell Society.

Retracing canals to Croydon and Camberwell. Living History 1988.

James S Dearden - *John Ruskin's Camberwell,* Brentham Press, 1990.

C F Dendy Marshall - *A History of the Southern Railway,* revised ed., Ian Allen, 1963.

Robert J Harley - *Camberwell and West Norwood tramways,* Middleton Press, 1993.

A descriptive account of Peckham and Camberwell illus., Robinson, and Pike, 1892.

S.Humphrey - *Camberwell, Dulwich and Peckham in old photographs,* Sutton, 1996.

The times of our lives 1900-1945, Peckham Publishing Project, 1983.

Old Ordnance Survey Maps; Camberwell and Stockwell, 1913; Peckham, 1914; Old Kent Road, 1894, 1914; Kennington and Walworth, 1870, 1914, Alan Godfrey.

4. IMPORTANT BUILDINGS

Joan Edmonds - *A brief account of the first 150 years of St George's, 1824-1974*

R A Ford - *A history of Camberwell Green Congregational Church, 1774-1966.*
Mary Boast - *St Giles, 1987,* Les Alden - *The East Window, 1992,* Friends of St Giles.
David Bryans - *St George's Primary School, Camberwell, 1826-1976.*
Gerald Broadribb - *Felix on the Bat,* Eyre & Spottiswoode, 1962.
The story of Mary Datchelor School, 1877-1977, Hodder & Stoughton, 1977.
Minutes of Camberwell Vestry, Camberwell Borough Council, London Borough of Southwark Council, and *Camberwell Board of Guardians*

5. ARTS AND ENTERTAINMENTS

Geoff Hassell - *Camberwell School of Arts and Crafts, 1943 - 1960,* 1995.
Giles Waterfield - *Art for the people.* Dulwich Picture Gallery, 1994.
Diana Howard - *London theatres and music halls, 1850-1950,* LA, 1970.
Malcolm Webb - *Amber Valley Gazetteer of Greater London's cinemas, 1946-86.*

6. THE TWENTIETH CENTURY

Camberwell Official Guide, 1916, 1921, and *Golden Jubilee Handbook,* 1950.
J M Filgate - *The history of the 33rd Divisional Artillery, 1914 - 1918,* Vacher, 1921
W J Hahn - *First Surrey Rifles; Festubert, 1915; Loos, 1915;* Typescripts.
The author later became Chief Librarian of Camberwell.
Hook, John - *The air raids on London 1914 - 1918 War; Booklet 14.* 2nd ed. 1989
Terry Norman - *The hell they called High Wood; the Somme 1916,* Stephens, 1984.
Lewis Blake - *Bolts from the blue; SE London and Kent under V2 rocket attack.* 1990
Civilian War Dead 1939-1945; Camberwell. Imperial War Graves Commission.
John Hook - *These rough notes; the raids on Southwark, part 2; Camberwell,* 1995.
Arthur B Woolf - *The battle of South London,* Crystal publications.
Incident registers, ARP, Home Guard and other *Civil Defence records.*
Rib Davis, ed., - *Southwark at War, memories and photographs,* L.B.S. 1996.
LBS Permanent Housing Estates, 1976. Also individual estates brochures.
Five Estates, 1993; *Peckham Partnership* 1994, L.B.Southwark.
Hunter Davies - *A walk round London's parks,* Hamilton, 1983, chap 10.
Burgess Park Walk, 1994; *Chumleigh Gardens,* 1995. L.B.Southwark leaflets.
David Solman - *Burgess Park tree and ecology survey,* Southwark Council, 1989.
Colin Rochester - *Cambridge House, the first hundred years, 1889-1989.*
Cambridge House; Talbot; St Giles Trust; Camberwell Circle; Lovewalk; - *Reports*
James A Heathcote - *The Platanes; a history of King's College Hall.* 1979.
Forty winters on; memories Caribbean immigrants, Lambeth Services. 1988.
Southwark Ward Profiles; from the 1991 Census, Southwark Council, 1993.
David A Vaughan - *Negro victory; the life story of Dr Harold Moody,* 1950.
West Indian Gazette, 1959-65, on microfilm at Lambeth Archives
Black Cultural Archives, 378 Coldharbour Lane, SW9 8LF.

7. POSTSCRIPT

D H Allport - *A Staffordshire Lad; Thomas Allport and his descendants, 1758 - 1966*
W H Blanch - *Camberwell,* enlarged by W F Noble, Vol. 1 p 7 Lambeth Archives.

Index

London Borough of Southwark Neighbourhood Histories
1. Camberwell
2. Dulwich
3. Peckham
4. Walworth
5. Bermondsey
6. Rotherhithe
7. 'The Borough'
8. Bankside